THE GIPPER'S GHOST

A STORY OF THE SPIRIT OF NOTRE DAME

By Robert A. Quakenbush

THE GIPPER'S GHOST
Cavalry Press Edition

DEDICATION

This Cavalry Press edition of THE GIPPER'S GHOST is dedicated to my beautiful and wonderful wife and all-time favorite registered nurse, Mary Beth, and my beautiful and wonderful daughter, Kelly.

Living with me, they have had little choice but to become great Notre Dame football fans ~ and also great Detroit Tigers baseball fans.

Living with them, I have easily become their biggest fan.

Go Irish!

And remember:

Respect Coach Knute Rockne's name.

It's pronounced Kuh-newt.

FOREWORD

IMAGINE

One great story about one very unique place. A wonderful school with a French name and Irish tradition as well as a charming mystique.

JE NE SAIS QUOI.

What undefinable and mysterious quality Notre Dame has by the carload, all captured twenty-nine years ago by a gifted writer named Bob Quakenbush, who created a Fighting Irish masterpiece. *The Gipper's Ghost* is now under consideration as a major motion picture, which will transfer this author's rich imagination and wonderful storytelling onto the large screen.

This story has it all — warmth, humor, and legends — but most of all it captures the author's love for Notre Dame and its spirit, a university immersed in a culture of excellence and founded on virtue and determination. While at all times respecting the customs and traditions of Our Lady's school, the author has created a Notre Dame football classic. Bob Quakenbush would be the first to agree that even without a football team (good heavens!) Notre Dame would still be the finest Catholic university on Planet Earth.

If you are a first time reader, you should be envied, as you are about to revel in a once-in-a-lifetime experience.

Shake down the Thunder.

Patrick Brent ND #29
Hawaii
17 March 2014

"WHAT THOUGH THE ODDS BE GREAT OR SMALL"

When *THE GIPPER'S GHOST* is made into a motion picture (What though the odds be great or small!), it is essential that the script for the film reflects the sum of the University of Notre Dame today, which is so very much more than the flickering images presented in old newsreels about the Fighting Irish football teams of yesteryear.

Three Hollywood movies have been made about Notre Dame; all three focused primarily on football. Since the era of Rockne and the Gipper, however, Notre Dame has evolved from an "all-male" college into a coeducational institution of higher education, and has risen to stand among the finest universities in the land. It is my hope than any script based on *THE GIPPER'S GHOST* will succeed in showcasing every facet of Notre Dame, including its Catholic heritage and character, outstanding academics and research, and vibrant student life. No stereotypical Hollywood fare, no gratuitous violence, just warmth, humor, and an engaging story about life, love, friendship, and football under the Golden Dome.

As the book's full title suggests, *THE GIPPER'S GHOST: A Story of the Spirit of Notre Dame* is really a story about the legendary and unquenchable spirit of Our Lady's University, using a football fable as a framework. Indeed, it has always been my belief that Father Edward Sorin, the University's founder, personally and single-handedly forged the indomitable spirit of Notre Dame in one bold and unforgettable moment in 1879 (a story told in Chapter 25).

Father Sorin's Golden Dome remains – as it always should be – the centerpiece of Notre Dame, but now the Dome is surrounded by a beautiful and photogenic college campus that is sure to be a cinematographer's delight. Just like in the book, a *THE GIPPER'S GHOST* movie will show audiences the most magnificent and inspiring places on campus, creating a special visual keepsake for the Notre Dame family, and allowing a new generation of moviegoers to discover exactly why Our Lady's University holds such a special place in the minds and hearts of her loyal sons and daughters.

Love thee, Notre Dame,

Robert A. Quakenbush
Notre Dame, Indiana
March 17, 2014

In the 1940 film, *Knute Rockne – All American*, the role of George Gipp was played by a young actor named Ronald Reagan. In the film version of *THE GIPPER'S GHOST*, who should play the Gipper?

Table of Contents

Chapter One: SHADOWS OVER THE DOME   1

Chapter Two: DIVINE INTERVENTION   5

Chapter Three: ROCKNE'S CHALLENGE   7

Chapter Four: ROCKNE'S PLAN   13

Chapter Five: THE BIG RED MACHINE   19

Chapter Six: A GLIMMER OF HOPE   25

Chapter Seven: THE GIPPER'S LEGEND   33

Chapter Eight: THE SPORTS EDITOR   41

Chapter Nine: TEN COMMANDMENTS OF NOTRE DAME 45

Chapter Ten: VICTORY AT LAST   49

Chapter Eleven: NICKI MAKES A PASS   55

Chapter Twelve: THE QUEST   61

Chapter Thirteen: KELLY'S PROMISE   67

Chapter Fourteen: GOD ONLY KNOWS   75

Chapter Fifteen: FOOTBALL SATURDAY   77

Chapter Sixteen: MIRACLE AT NOTRE DAME   81

Chapter Seventeen: THE GIPPER'S GHOST   87

Chapter Eighteen: WOMAN'S INTUITION   91

Chapter Nineteen: AN INVITATION   95

Chapter Twenty: NICKI'S DISCOVERY   99

Chapter Twenty-One: RESTORING THE LUSTRE   103

Chapter Twenty-Two: OUT FOR THE SEASON   107

Chapter Twenty-Three: WHAT THOUGH THE ODDS   109

Chapter Twenty-Four: ND'S GREATEST RIVAL   115

Chapter Twenty-Five: THE SPIRIT OF NOTRE DAME   119

EPILOG   129

ABOUT THE AUTHOR   131

EXPLANATORY NOTES   133

Chapter One: SHADOWS OVER THE DOME

No more timeouts for the Fighting Irish.

Hart Collins called his own number and scrambled to the Michigan 18 yard line. The Irish offense regrouped, and the sophomore quarterback flicked a 10 yard pass to Ryan O'Connor. O'Connor fought off the Wolverine defender and slipped out of bounds to stop the clock at 0:06.

Collins took a deep breath. Again, the ball was snapped. He rifled a bullet to O'Connor at the goal line. The ball skittered off his fingertips.

Two seconds left.

Back in the huddle, Collins called the same play.

The snap...the throw...TOUCHDOWN NOTRE DAME!

The Irish had averted an opening day shutout. The extra point narrowed the final score to Michigan 45, Notre Dame 7.

In the post-game interview room, Joe Kelly dutifully answered the questions of a scornful press. At 38, Kelly was everything the nation's sportswriters had come to expect in a Notre Dame head coach. Irish. Catholic. And a loser.

"Notre Dame's been playing football for more than a century now," sniped John Thornton, the well-known sports columnist of the Chicago Tribune. "By rights, the Fighting Irish should be contenders

1

for the national championship. Instead, they're the doormats of college football. What happened this time?"

Thornton's colleague from Blue & Gold Illustrated, a once-popular Notre Dame fan magazine which had recently filed for Chapter Eleven, chimed in, "Who's at fault, Coach? Your players? Your assistant coaches? You?"

From below, the muffled sounds of the Notre Dame Victory March filtered into the room as the marching band exited through the stadium's north tunnel. Kelly thought to himself that an Irish lullaby might be more appropriate.

Rising from their seats in the highest level of Notre Dame Stadium's press box, Father Patrick Romano, president of the university, Father Matt Cockrell, executive vice president in charge of athletics, and William "Wild Bill" Fallon, the athletic director, appeared uniformly shame-faced. As they grimly donned their raincoats, they knew tonight's special reception for distinguished alumni would not be pleasant.

They would, of course, maintain dignity by pointing with pride to the Notre Dame athletic department's most hallowed statistic: that 98 percent of the school's student-athletes earned their diplomas. And all three men would affirm the administration's faith in Joe Kelly.

Besides, Joe Kelly still had three years left on his contract.

In the locker room, Hart Collins was inconsolable. Many of his teammates had already showered, yet he still wore what remained

2

of his uniform. His tattered blue jersey sported a new, sleeveless look invented 40 minutes earlier by a particularly aggressive Michigan linebacker. His gold helmet shone dully underneath the fluorescent light; it was spattered with mud from the third of five sacks he had endured.

Hart Collins had been unaccustomed to losing during his "glory years" as an all-state quarterback at Birmingham Brother Rice, a suburban Catholic high school on the outskirts of Detroit. The Brother Rice Warriors had been undefeated state champions during his junior and senior seasons. His dad had been so proud of the two touchdowns he had scored in the title game his senior year.

Hart wondered what his dad must be thinking now. Today, he had thrown three interceptions – all to the same Wolverine linebacker. Coach Kelly's concession that the Michigan defender had been the only man open all day offered little consolation.

Indeed, had the Fighting Irish of Notre Dame forgotten how to win?

Overhead, the sound of thunder shattered the autumn calm. A bolt of lightning raked across the Indiana skies.

In Heaven, a frustrated and angry God – Self-proclaimed as Notre's Dame's "Number One Fan" – decided His divine intervention was more than a little overdue.

He issued a memo.

Chapter Two: DIVINE INTERVENTION

A bewildered soul in a gray sweatsuit reported to the Lord's office a short time later. He knocked and entered.

Flashing a lopsided smile, he said, "I got your memo, Sir. I came right away." One usually didn't keep The Boss waiting.

God closed the book he had been examining. The visitor noted the words, Permanent Record, inlaid in gold on its cover.

God spoke, "You're aware of the Notre Dame situation, aren't you?" he asked.

The soul answered. "Yes, sir. I am. Twenty-two straight losses. You know how much I love Notre Dame. I never would have left, except..."

God interrupted, "I know, I know. But I needed you up here. The guardian angels were experiencing a mid-eternity crisis. Morale was low and you were the best motivational speaker available."

The Lord returned to the issue at hand.

"My son, Catholic football in America is in a shambles. It's a sin how many Catholic high schools are changing their nicknames from the Fighting Irish to such devilish variations as the Blue Demons. That pagan team in Southern California has stolen the national collegiate championship two years in a row. It has to stop!

"Mind you, never before have I directly intervened in a Notre Dame football game, despite rumors to the contrary. But I really am a fan. And I confess I do take secret pleasure in those bumper stickers I've spotted on the Indiana Toll Road. You know, the ones that say 'God Made Notre Dame Number One.' They're usually found on the rusted-out bumpers of 1977 Chevrolets*.

"But surely you realize that I didn't make Notre Dame 'Number One' that year or any other year. The boys did it themselves. Oh, sure, I admit I may have stopped that 15 miles-per-hour wind at precisely the right moment at the end of the 1980 Michigan game. But give Harry Oliver most of the credit. He's the one who actually kicked the ball 51 yards!"

"That was quite the miracle finish, Sir," the soul in the sweatshirt acknowledged. "Having no time remaining on the clock was a nice touch, too."

"Lately, however," God resumed, "I have been preoccupied with other problems. You know how it is. If it isn't the Russians, it's the Democrats. Fortunately, Heaven admitted its first management consultant just the other day. She's given me quite a few pointers already about effective delegation."

"And so, Knute, I'm delegating! I'm returning you to Notre Dame. Your assignment is to resurrect a winning tradition at Our Lady's University!!!"

Chapter Three: ROCKNE'S CHALLENGE

The soul of Knute Rockne was stunned. Although he had thoroughly enjoyed his heavenly reward, he had been a bit miffed when the Lord drafted him into The Biggest League of All on that fateful day in March, 1931*.

A chance to go back to Notre Dame...

"...of course, Knute, anything or anyone you need will be at your immediate disposal." God's commanding voice brought Rockne back to attention.

Being a soul of action, he made a swift decision.

"I want George to go with me."

God leaned back. At last count, there were 128,912 souls named George listed in the Permanent Record. "George?"

"George Gipp," Rockne answered.

God was a little surprised. Knute usually played by the rules. "Knute, you know he's ineligible. He's still in Purgatory working off all those misspent afternoons in South Bend's pool halls...when he should have been studying!"

"It's a tough assignment, Lord," countered Rockne. "I need the Gipper."

God relented.

"Oh, I suppose it can be arranged. Tell you what. I'll even fix it so that he receives a certain amount of plenary indulgences for every touchdown he scores while wearing a Notre Dame uniform. They'll be credited to his account in the Permanent Record."

"Thank you, Sir. When do we start?"

"The next time someone lights a candle for the football team at the Grotto, you're on your way. Good luck, Knute!"

Rockne's spirit rose. He started to leave.

"Wait, Knute. I almost forgot!"

The Lord handed Rockne two large tablets made of stone.

"I wrote these during halftime of today's game. Deliver them for me," said the Lord.

Win or lose, Joe Kelly was an exceptionally devout Catholic. As was his custom after every game, he made a visit to the Grotto of Our Lady of Lourdes to say a rosary in honor of the Blessed Virgin. The Grotto, a one-seventh scale replica of the original French shrine, had been built in 1896. It had become one of the most beloved spots at Notre Dame. Generations of Notre Dame men and women had offered fervent prayers at the site.

Kelly knelt at his usual spot along the rail, near the statue of Saint Bernadette. He had to smile. An earlier visitor, probably one of the co-eds, had placed fresh flowers in the statue's delicate left hand.

He prayed the Rosary, and then added an extra Hail Mary. He hoped the Lord occasionally listened to a coach's prayer.

Kelly rose to leave, then turned back and entered the Grotto. He removed two quarters from his pocket and slid them through the slot of the collection box. Taking a taper, he touched its waxed end to one of the burning flames. He lit a devotional candle in the back row, where it was a little more sheltered from the wind.

As he strode resolutely from the Grotto toward his office at the Athletic and Convocation Center, he was already too preoccupied with next Saturday's game with Michigan State to notice the flash of heavenly light over his shoulder.

Rockne and Gipp landed on a bench at the edge of the clearing. They observed Coach Kelly as he headed away.

"That's him, poor soul." said Rockne, "Joe Kelly. A Notre Dame alumnus and a fine man, too. This is his third season at Notre Dame. He came here determined to turn the Notre Dame program around. He knew it would be difficult, and it hasn't been easy on him. But he loves the University of Notre Dame."

"Do you really think we can help him, Rock?" asked Gipp.

"I'm not sure, Gipper. But we'll certainly give it the old college try!"

Rockne suggested a tour of the campus. Gipp enthusiastically agreed. Like other souls assigned temporary guardian angel duty, they were invisible to mortals until they chose to reveal themselves.

Therefore, they could move undetected among the passing parade of priests, professors, students and alumni.

Rockne and Gipp walked up the steps to the left of the Grotto and circled behind Sacred Heart Church. Passing the east entrance, Rockne told Gipp that the Gothic passageway had been added to the church in the 1920s as a memorial to Notre Dame students who perished in World War I. Carved into the stone above the door was the motto: "God. Country. Notre Dame."

Entering the Main Quad, the souls turned and looked upward.

The Golden Dome, high atop the university's Administration Building, was the centerpiece of Notre Dame. The 19-foot statue of Our Lady which rested on its peak had reigned above the beautifully-landscaped campus for more than a century.

"She's still a lovely sight," Rock, said Gipp. "The gold leaf looks as good as new."

The central campus was much as Rockne and Gipp remembered. Many of the buildings surrounding the perimeter of the Main Quad had been standing during their era. Most had aged gracefully. Ivy now covered their exterior walls.

Suddenly, Rockne grew excited. There was one thing he wanted to see!

"C'mon, George. Follow me!"

They walked briskly southeast and crossed the South Quad. When they emerged from the walkways between the Hall of

Engineering and O'Shaughnessy Hall, Rockne's destination came into full view.

Notre Dame Stadium!

"The House That Rockne Built" was an impressive structure. It had been built during the Golden Age of Sports by the same construction firm responsible for Comiskey Park in Chicago and Yankee Stadium in New York. Its outer wall stood 45 feet high and measured a half-mile in circumference. Along its rim fluttered brightly-colored pennants symbolic of Notre Dame and its opponents for the season.

Rockne said, "George, I coached the Irish to a 20 to 14 win over Southern Methodist on opening day in October, 1930. What a day! I wished you could have been there!"

"So do I!"

Rockne glanced at Gipp, suddenly remembering. Their eyes, glistening with tears, met. Both realized how much they missed being part of Notre Dame.

Together, they made a silent vow to restore the lustre to its golden tradition.

Chapter Four: ROCKNE'S PLAN

That evening, Rockne and Gipp lounged in the LaFortune Student Center.

Rockne leafed through the previous day's edition of The Observer, the daily student newspaper. An article on the sports page triggered an idea. Notre Dame's interhall football season would begin the next day.

"George, I think I've found a way to showcase your skills for our good friend, Coach Kelly."

"What's that, Rock?"

"I want you to play in an interhall game tomorrow afternoon. If you play as well as you used to, you should be a walk-on member of the varsity by Monday morning. With any luck at all, you'll make the traveling squad to East Lansing next weekend."

"Sounds like a good plan, Rock. Which team should I play for?"

"Well, I thought you might enjoy playing for Sorin, your old residence hall," said Rockne, for a couple of reasons. One, it's one of the smallest men's dorms on campus. They could use a good player against Dillon. Otherwise, they'll get slaughtered. Two, it's home to Hart Collins, your new roommate."

13

"The Irish quarterback?"

"Precisely."

"But that means I'll have to be a student..."

"Precisely."

"Now wait just a minute, Rock..."

"Too late, George, it's all arranged. God's already taken care of most of the paperwork. All we need to do is give you a new name."

"I almost didn't think of that, Rock. You're right. I'll need an alias. I can't just walk into Sorin Hall with a duffel bag, walk into Hart's room, leap onto the top bunk and say 'Hello, I'm your new roommate. By the way, my name is George Gipp.' He'll die laughing."

"More likely he'll die of fright. He'll think he's met a ghost!" Rockne said.

Suddenly, Gipp chuckled. He had an idea. He had read an article on The Observer's front page about a former United States president.

"How about Dutch Reagan?"

'Rockne started to protest, "But that's the former president's name..."

"Fair's fair, Rock. He borrowed my nickname with some success. Besides, I hear he has a wonderful sense of humor. I don't think he'll mind.

Rockne considered Gipp's suggestion. He remembered his recent chat with Pat O'Brien, bless his soul, who had been a good

14

friend of Mr. Reagan while on earth. Pat spoke very well of the former president.

"No, I suppose he won't. He is Irish, after all."

"Then it's settled. Dutch Reagan it is. Now, what about your disguise, Rock?"

"All taken care of, George. It's perfect. You won't believe it."

Later that night, Hart Collins was surprised to see the lights on under his door. He was sure he had turned them off before heading over to the Morris Inn to have dinner with his parents, who had driven down from Detroit for the game. The Morris Inn was a small hotel operated by the university. It was located near the university's main entrance.

So, he was understandably curious when he stepped inside the room and discovered someone stretched out on the top bunk.

"Hi, I'm your new roommate. Dutch Reagan's the name."

Then Collins remembered. Father Sinon, the hall rector, had mentioned earlier in the week that Collins could expect a new roommate any day now. Father Sinon had explained that an unusually high acceptance rate had resulted in overcrowded conditions in the university's residence halls. Some of the freshmen assigned to the towers, Flanner Hall and Grace Hall, had been forced to live in hastily-converted study lounges, sharing space with as many as five roommates. The students often referred to these arrangements as "six-packs."

The priest had told Collins that some of the students were being shifted to other dorms to alleviate the overcrowding.

"Hello, Dutch. Welcome to Sorin. Where have you been living?"

Gipp thought fast. "I've been staying off campus." It was close enough to the truth.

"Oh, I forgot to introduce myself. My name is Hart Collins."

"I know. You're a pretty good quarterback."

"Come on, Dutch, who are you kidding? Michigan killed us today. The Wolverines are laughing all the way back to Ann Arbor." Collins was still dejected from the day's events.

"No, seriously. I'm from Michigan, too." Now that, thought Gipp, was the truth. He had grown up in Michigan's Upper Peninsula. "I know you set a lot of records at Brother Rice. They say you were the best quarterback at Brother Rice since Al Fracassa coached there!"

"It seems hard to believe now," muttered Collins.

"I'll bet you're still that good. Don't be so hard on yourself. You didn't get much playing time last year as a freshman, but now that you've been named the starting quarterback..."

"That's just part of Coach Kelly's long-range rebuilding program. He hopes we can play .500 ball my senior year."

Gipp thought, "This guy really is discouraged."

16

"Hart, what's that plaque hanging on the wall, next to the Detroit Tigers pennant?"

Collins walked over to the plaque, an award he had received in high school for his leadership as a varsity athlete.

"One of the early athletic directors at Brother Rice started giving this award out. It's one of my favorite possessions. Whenever things are really rough, whenever I read a negative story in the press or hear boos from the home crowd or receive an angry letter from a disgruntled alumnus, I'll often read this. It's a quote from Theodore Roosevelt."

"What does it say?" Dutch asked.

"It's pretty long."

"That's O.K. I'm not going anywhere. Read the whole thing."

Collins began reading the inscription aloud, "It is not the critic who counts; not the man who points out how the strong man stumbled, or where the doer of a deed could have done better. The credit belongs to the man who is actually in the arena, whose face is marred by dust and sweat and blood, who strives valiantly, who errs and comes short again and again because there is no effort without error and shortcoming. It is the man who does actually strive to do the deeds, who knows the great enthusiasms, the great devotions, who spends himself in a worthy cause, who at the best knows in the end the triumph of high achievement, and who at the worst, if he fails, at least fails while daring greatly, so that his place will never be with those cold and timid souls who know neither victory nor defeat."

17

Dutch said softly, "Hart, I think the Fighting Irish may do very well this year."

Collins appreciated the thought, but decided to change the subject. The new roommates talked for a few more minutes, but as it was already quite late, they decided to turn in for the night.

As Gipp turned out the lights, he said, "By the way, I'm going to play in the interhall game tomorrow. Why don't you come on out and cheer your new roommate on to victory?"

"Victory? Against Dillon Hall?" Collins thought to himself, This Reagan kid sure doesn't know much about football. "Say good night, Dutch."

Collins drifted into sleep.

Chapter Five: THE BIG RED MACHINE

Interhall football at Notre Dame had a tradition of its own. On most other college campuses, intramural teams played touch football. Not Notre Dame. They played real football. Tackle football. Interhall players wore pads, helmets, uniforms, mouth guards and game-faces.

A number of students firmly believed that Notre Dame's best interhall team could play competitively against many small college football teams. The entire student body, at least for the moment, was absolutely convinced they could beat the Notre Dame varsity. Easily.

Interhall football featured nicknames such as the Holy Cross Hogs, the Grace Tower Gorillas and the Stanford Studs. The "Notre Dame" of Notre Dame – the team every interhall player dreamed of beating at least once during his lifetime – was Dillon's Hall's "Big Red Machine." Dillon Hall was the ultimate "jock" dorm on campus; the unmistakable aroma of sweat socks penetrated every room and corridor of the hall. The perennial South Quad champions, Dillon Hall had lost only once in the past four years. The defeat had arrived in a championship game against the North Quad's superpower, Keenan Hall.

This year's Dillon Hall squad was, as usual, the preseason favorite to win it all. According to the sports editor of The Observer, Dillon had recruited five high school All-Americans for its offensive line alone!

Sorin Hall didn't have a prayer.

Gipp had been carrying his helmet when he passed the bleachers set up next to the field. He spotted Collins in the top row.

With a wave of his helmet, Gipp called, "Hart! Thanks for coming!"

"I promised I would. Do you really think our brave but tiny hall has a chance against these guys?" He pointed in the general direction of the red-shirted barbarians on the opposite sideline. "Dillon has all-state players from Ohio, Pennsylvania, Texas..."

"Don't worry, Hart," said Gipp with a smile, "they don't have me!"

Collins laughed with him.

Meanwhile, in the football office on the first floor of the Athletic and Convocation Center – popularly known as the A.C.C. – Joe Kelly was deep in thought. He had been studying the depth charts, searching for a magic combination that might yield a glimmer of hope against the powerful Michigan State Spartans.

He didn't notice the priest who had entered his office.

"Oh, Coach! Sorry. Didn't mean to disturb you. I was just nosing around a bit."

Kelly looked up. "That's O.K., Father. It's quite all right," he said. He had no reason to be suspicious. Who questioned the presence of a priest anywhere at Notre Dame?

"If you don't mind me saying so, Coach, you look exhausted. Why don't you just relax for a little while? There's a football game starting up outside. Why don't you take an hour or two and watch the kids play? After all, Sunday is a day of rest. And who knows, maybe you'll even discover the next George Gipp!"

Kelly smiled. "You're probably right, Father. The fresh air might do me some good at that. Care to join me?"

Kelly and the priest took a shortcut through the north dome of the A.C.C. They strolled over to the bleachers. The game had started.

Kelly saw Hart Collins, and climbed up to join him.

"Looking for some new receivers?" Kelly asked.

"Not really, Coach. I promised my roommate I'd watch him play today."

"I don't think I've met your roommate. Which one is he?"

Suddenly, there was a roar from the Sorin Hall cheering section.

"That one!" said Collins, jumping to his feet.

On the field, Dutch Reagan had just ricocheted off two Dillon linebackers. He accelerated toward the end zone, 10 yards ahead of

21

this nearest pursuers. They were 20 yards behind when he nimbly crossed the goal line.

For the next hour, Kelly and Collins witnessed the dismantling of the "Big Red Machine." The best interhall athletes played both ways, and Gipp, who had learned the game during an era of single-platoon football, proved sensational. On offense, he led Sorin in rushing, receiving and scoring. On defense, he led in tackles, sacks and interceptions. He might have led in punting, too, but as it turned out, Sorin Hall never had occasion to punt.

Kelly thought it was probably the most awesome display of individual football prowess at Notre Dame since, well, the days of George Gipp!

At game's end, Collins and the men of Sorin Hall charged onto the field. They carried their new hero on their shoulders in a triumphant, boisterous march to St. Joseph's Lake, all the while chanting, "Lake! Lake!" In a time-honored ceremony, the celebrants christened their champion by hurling him off the pier into the chilly September waters.

Meanwhile, back at the A.C.C., Kelly's mind raced with the possibilities.

"He's quite a boy, isn't he, Coach?"

It was the priest again.

"He just might be the answer to a prayer, Father," said Kelly.

Kelly was about to offer to take his new friend to dinner, when he realized he didn't even know his name.

"Are you just visiting Notre Dame, Father...?"

The priest understood.

"Woulfe. Father Michael B. Woulfe. Sort of. Actually, I'm on assignment from the Vatican."

"The Vatican! It must be an important assignment."

"It is, Joe, it is. I'm your new team chaplain."

"Chaplain?!!!?"

"Joe, when a chaplain loses 22 in a row with all the talent available at Notre Dame, it's about time he got replaced, don't you think? The Pope certainly did. So here I am. Or would you prefer a coaching change?"

"Who am I to question the decisions of the Pope? Besides, any priest who helps me find a halfback like that deserves to be promoted to head chaplain at Notre Dame! Welcome aboard, Father Woulfe!"

"You can call me by my nickname. My friends call me Father Rock."

The Lord was right, thought Rockne. A Roman collar at Notre Dame is a perfect disguise.

Even the toupee fit.

Chapter Six: A GLIMMER OF HOPE

Hart Collins was absent from practice most of this week. So was Mike Samick, the first string center. Pressed by concerned coaches and players to explain their absence, Joe Kelly said only, "They're working on a secret weapon," without elaborating further.

Actually, while the rest of the Fighting Irish were sweating, sprinting and straining on the artificial turf of Cartier Field, Collins, Samick and the newly-recruited walk-on, Dutch Reagan, were hard at work. Each afternoon, Father Rock drove the three young men to a secluded high school practice field in South Bend, where they rehearsed passing plays until sundown. Rockne told Gipp the sessions reminded him of the summer he and Gus Dorais had spent at Cedar Point perfecting the forward pass that had jolted a presumably invincible 1913 Army team and put little-known Notre Dame on the map.

The secrecy was maintained on Friday, when Father Rock and his charges made the trip to East Lansing by car instead of taking the team plane.

The Notre Dame-Michigan State rivalry had been a fierce one characterized by hard hitting and close scores. The closest of all had been the famous 10-10 tie in 1966. Ara Parseghian's Irish and Duffy

Daugherty's Spartans had both been undefeated and ranked No. 1 and No. 2, respectively, in the polls. The tie had cost Michigan State a second straight national championship, which Notre Dame claimed outright in its season finale by overwhelming USC 51-0.

In recent years, the Spartans had dominated the series. At the outset of the game, the trend seemed certain to continue.

The Irish backfield committed two mortal sins in the first quarter, fumbling the ball twice deep in Notre Dame territory. The Spartans seized both opportunities. Two field goals established a six point advantage.

Notre Dame's receivers noticed the change in Hart Collins first. Collins was really zipping the ball today. Unfortunately, their perception had been better than their reception. Virtually all of Collins' passes had been right in their hands. If they hadn't dropped four of them, the Irish probably would have held a slim lead.

Nevertheless, in the huddle Collins remained cool, confident and relaxed, despite the frustration of the early setbacks. At one point during the second quarter, he calmly announced, "Gentlemen, our losing streak ends today."

The Irish moved the ball successfully during the second quarter. Although they failed to score, they did manage a series of impressive first downs. The Spartans' only scoring threat was foiled when the Irish free safety, Shenandoah Lee, leaped high into the air to swat down a pass destined for the end zone.

At halftime, the score stood at MSU 6-ND 0.

In the locker room, Kelly took Collins and Reagan aside.

"Ready, boys?"

"Ready, sir."

"Dutch, when Hart gives you the ball, you just run with it."

"How far?"

The second half started miserably for the Irish. The Spartans returned the kickoff for a touchdown. To add insult to injury, they decided to go for two.

MSU 14-ND 0.

Shenandoah Lee fielded the ensuing kickoff for the Irish, and fought his way to the Notre Dame 28. The Notre Dame offense took the field.

Few of the sportswriters seemed aware that a new halfback had entered the game for the Irish. John Thornton of the Chicago Tribune observed the new player didn't even have a name sewn on his jersey. He assumed "Mr. Nice Guy" Kelly was probably giving a local boy some playing time in front of friends and family. He returned his attention to WGN-TV's broadcast of the Chicago Cubs baseball game, which he had tuned in on his battery-powered Sony Watchman.

Collins introduced the new halfback to the Irish offense. "This is Dutch Reagan. He promised my mother he'd look after me. She's been concerned about my health since those five sacks you gentlemen permitted last week."

At the line of scrimmage, Collins called his own number. He followed Reagan through the line for a six yard gain. There was an official timeout while the Spartan trainers assisted Michigan State's giant middle linebacker, Bubba Angstrom, from the field.

"Good blocking, Dutch!"

Reagan was next. He smashed through the center of the line for a first down.

Three more plays. Three more clouds of dust. Another first down.

Three more plays, including a quick one over the middle to Ryan O'Connor, left the Irish with a fourth and two. Reagan punted for the corner. His kick was downed on the Spartans' two yard line.

Unimpressed, the Spartans bullied their way to the 23, but an inspired Notre Dame defense forced them to surrender the ball. The punt was high, but short. Lee signaled for a fair catch. The ND offense returned with excellent field position.

On the first play of the series, Reagan sprinted out of the backfield. Collins rolled out, cocked and fired. First down!

Next play. Collins dropped back. Reagan threw a brush block, then drifted toward the sideline. O'Connor raced down the near side.

Green Spartan jerseys converged on Collins. At the last second, he flipped the ball to Reagan, who launched a missile to the end zone.

O'Connor left the ground at the goal line. The ball had been slightly overthrown...two inches, at most. He stretched his arms and clutched the ball. He somersaulted through the end zone, yet somehow retained control of the football.

As if in blessing, the referee raised his arms.

MSU 14-ND 6.

Reagan took a handoff from Collins and went airborne for the two-point conversion.

MSU 14-ND 8.

The Spartans wisely chose to keep the ball on the ground after that, grinding out yardage and erasing minutes from the clock. The blowout they had anticipated had failed to materialize, but they still had the lead and had every intention of protecting it.

But the Fighting Irish were equally aroused. O'Connor's touchdown had inspired the defense. They bent but didn't break under repeated Spartan attacks.

The teams traded possessions until midway through the fourth quarter. Collins turned a broken play into a 40 yard gain. The drive stalled at the Spartan 15, so Coach Kelly called on freshman placekicker Tom Roberts. Robert's field goal attempt split the uprights.

MSU 14-ND 11.

On the sideline, Joe Kelly turned to Father Rock.

"What do you think, Father? Think we have a chance to win?"

"I don't know, Joe. Spartans have hated losing ever since that incident at Thermopylae. For your sake, I hope so. One loss is good for the soul. Too many losses is not good for the coach."

Late in the fourth quarter, disaster struck. A blitzing linebacker forced Collins to fumble. Michigan State recovered, and the Spartans ripped off two long gainers.

With the sudden change in momentum, the Spartan quarterback, King Leonidas, got cocky. He sensed the Irish had returned to normal. His favorite receiver had beaten his coverage by a mile on the last play.

As he moved to take the snap from center, he failed to notice that the Irish had made a substitution on defense.

Leonidas hurled the ball deep as visions of touchdowns and an NFL rookie contract danced in his head.

Dutch Reagan, now playing defense, matched his target step for step. He spun and intercepted the ball. He made it back to the Notre Dame 47 before five Spartans wrestled him to the ground.

On the sideline, Rockne wasn't at all surprised. One of the remarkable things about Gipp during his earlier playing days was that he had never allowed a pass completion in his territory. Never.

There was time for one more play. The Irish set up for a field goal attempt.

In the press box, the sportswriters were astonished. John Thornton stifled a laugh. He could see that Collins was the holder,

30

and that the "nameless wonder" was filling in for Tom Roberts, the kicker.

"It's a trick play. Collins will throw it as far as he can and pray a Hail Mary," he said to no one in particular.

"Yeah, it's gotta be a bomb," came a reply.

The Spartans certainly thought so. Their pass-prevent defense was well-deployed.

Up in Heaven, God drew a deep breath.

The wind stopped. The American flag hung limply on the flagpole.

Kneeling seven yards behind the line of scrimmage, Collins looked up at Reagan and called out a final reminder.

"Remember what the coach said, Dutch. Concentrate! Approach. Impact. Follow-through!"

"I'll remember. I'm ready."

Collins fielded the snap and placed the ball on the tee in one continuous motion. Reagan stepped forward and kicked.

The football soared heavenward, peaked and began its descent.

It just might be long enough.

The ball hit the crossbar...

...and bounced over!!

The electronic scoreboard displayed the outcome. The clock read 0:00. Home 14, Visitors 14.

Collins embraced Reagan. Notre Dame's losing streak had ended. In a tie.

Chapter Seven: THE GIPPER'S LEGEND

Joe Kelly slept well Saturday night. He rose early, slipped on his bathrobe and slippers and tiptoed downstairs. He let Rusty, the family's golden retriever, out the front door. Rusty bounded to the end of the driveway, scooped up the Sunday paper in his teeth and galloped back inside.

"Good boy, Rusty," Kelly said, "trading a pair of Milkbones for the South Bend Tribune. He noticed that the Tribune had returned to its old practice of featuring a full-color game photo on the front page. Tucking the paper under his arm, he walked into the kitchen. His wife, Maureen, had been up for an hour. She was sewing.

"I'm on the letter 'G' already. Only two more to go," she said. She had been introduced to Dutch after the game, and had told him she thought it was a shame the equipment manager hadn't found time to add his name to his road jersey. She would personally make sure that everyone in Notre Dame Stadium this Saturday knew that the blue jersey with the numeral '1' belonged to Dutch Reagan.

"That's great, honey. Dutch will certainly appreciate it."

Maureen asked the question that so many interviewers had asked him the day before.

"Joe, where did you find that boy?"

Kelly explained. "The credit really belongs to one of the priests at Notre Dame. He wandered into my office last Sunday. He told me to go out and watch an intramural game. Dutch was playing for the Sorin Hall team. He was incredible!"

"Have I met this priest?"

"No, but you will. He's our new team chaplain. His name is Father Rock."

"Well, next time I visit you in the A.C.C., I'm going to find this Father Rock and give him a great big kiss on behalf of the Kellys."

"You're a sweetheart, Maureen."

"I know. Now go wake up the kids or we'll be late for church."

"Yes, coach. Right away, coach," he said. Maureen called the plays at home. He called Rusty. "Rusty! Upstairs! Go get the kids out of bed."

The dog accepted his new assignment with a joyful bark and raced up the stairway with Kelly on his tail.

Hart Collins was having a pleasant Sunday also. He barely made it to the 11:00 a.m. High Mass at Sacred Heart Church. The chapel choir was just finishing the entrance song when he slid quietly into one of the back pews.

Every few minutes, he sneaked a glance up at the choir loft. His girlfriend, Lauren Kennedy, sang in the choir.

After Mass, he and Lauren enjoyed a leisurely lunch at the South Dining Hall. Later, he spent part of the afternoon playing Frisbee with friends on the South Quad. The lush green lawns may have belonged to the groundskeepers on weekdays, but on weekends they were the property of the students. Unless the automatic sprinklers were turned on.

In the evening, he let Dutch persuade him to attend the annual screening of the Warner Bros. motion picture, Knute Rockne – All American, at the Knights of Columbus Hall. The movie starred Pat O'Brien as Knute Rockne and Ronald Reagan as George Gipp. Dutch had been strangely eager to see it.

But that night, so was Collins, even though by his own admission he had probably seen it seven times before.

After the show, Hart and Dutch decided to grab something to eat at the campus snack shop, "The Huddle." Hart ordered for both: Huddle-burgers with cheese, French fries and Coca-Cola Classic.

They occupied an empty booth. When Dutch sipped his Coke, he thought to himself, Now, this is the real thing. I'm glad at least some things never change around here.

Dutch was quite pleased with the film portrayal of himself. He couldn't resist the opportunity to bask a little longer in his own glory. "That George Gipp was sure some football player, wasn't he? I'll bet Ronald Reagan won an Academy Award for his performance."

Collins said, "Well, Ronald Reagan may deserve one for some of his more recent performances, but in 1940 the Oscar for best actor went to Jimmy Stewart for The Philadelphia Story." In addition to being a movie buff, Collins had won Sorin Hall's Trivial Pursuit championship last semester.

"I'm impressed, Mr. Trivia Expert. Tell me more about this Gipp fellow."

"Well, it's pretty much like it was in the film, although you know how Hollywood sometimes takes creative license with actual historical details. Gipp played for Knute Rockne, and most experts agree he was Notre Dame's greatest player. He was about your size, Dutch, six foot, 180 pounds.

"Anyway, during his final season, he contracted a strep throat infection. That was pretty serious in those days, medical care not being up to modern standards. I heard somewhere that the entire student body kept vigil outside St. Joseph's Hospital, praying for his recovery. But he died – only two weeks after he was named an All American.

"That was in December, 1920. The legend was born several years later, in 1928 – Rockne's worst season.

"There were 90,000 people on hand at Yankee Stadium for this game – one of the largest crowds ever to watch a sporting event in New York City. Very few felt the Irish had a chance of winning.

"Now, in the movie Rockne makes his great speech at halftime, but that's pure Hollywood. Apparently, the scriptwriter thought it would be more dramatic to have the Irish trailing at halftime."

"So, what actually happened?" Dutch asked.

Collins said, "Rockne really told the story before the game. The actual words probably varied a bit, but essentially he said what was presented in the film." Collins knew the speech by heart; he had memorized it as an exercise for his high school public speaking course. He imitated Pat O'Brien's rendition of Rockne's voice.

"Well, boys. I haven't a thing to say. You played a great game this first half, all of you. I guess we just can't win 'em all. Boys, I'm going to tell you something I've kept to myself for years. None of you here knew George Gipp. He was long before your time. But you all do know what his tradition stands for at Notre Dame. Well, the last thing he said to me was: 'Rock, sometime when the team is up against it, when things are wrong and the breaks are beating the boys, tell them to go in there with all they've got, and win just one for the Gipper. I don't know where I'll be then, Rock, he said. But I'll know about it, and I'll be happy.' That's all, boys."

"What a great speech," Dutch said.

"It worked. Supposedly there wasn't a dry eye in the locker room. Even the mayor of New York, who was in the locker room at the time, had tears in his eyes. It was a scoreless tie at the half. In the third quarter, Army scored a touchdown, but missed the extra point. The Irish finally scored when Jack Chevigny, one of Notre Dame's halfbacks, vaulted into the end zone for a touchdown. When he jumped back on his feet, he threw the ball in the air and said, 'That's one for the Gipper!' He really said it!"

37

Collins went on. "Anyway, the Irish missed the extra point, so the score stood at 6-6 at the end of the third quarter. Late in the game, the Irish had a third and 26 at the Army 32. Frank Carideo hit Johnny O'Brien with a touchdown pass to make it 12-6. That lead almost didn't hold up. Army made it to the Notre Dame one yard line. A goal line defense stopped the Cadets there just as the final gun sounded to end the game."

"What a finish!" said Gipp.

"Perhaps more accurately, what a beginning for the legend of the Gipper. The following Monday a feature story in the New York Daily News revealed the story. The headline said, GIPP'S GHOST BEATS ARMY. IRISH HERO'S DEATHBED REQUEST INSPIRED NOTRE DAME. When Warner Bros. made the movie in 1940, "Win one for the Gipper" became part of the American language. It's been used at pep rallies and political rallies ever since."

"Has anyone ever equaled Gipp?" asked Gipp. He was understandably curious. News traveled slowly in Purgatory.

"Most of his statistics have been surpassed on the field. His rushing record of 2,341 yards held up for more than half a century. But no one has ever matched his legend. Wherever he is, he should be proud of himself."

Dutch Reagan said quietly, "I'm sure he is. Thanks for the story, Hart."

"You know the most amazing part of the Gipp story, though? He never played football in high school. He preferred baseball. He was an excellent centerfielder. After graduation, he planned to play for the Chicago Cubs."

Chapter Eight: THE SPORTS EDITOR

Monday evening, Dutch and his teammates enjoyed steaks in the North Dining Hall. Real, "training table" steaks, not the "mystery meat" variety customarily served to the school's student population.

Hart Collins found a discarded copy of The Observer on a nearby table. He began reading "Summer's Sports," the daily column written by the sports editor.

"What does Summers have to say about the game?"

Collins read from the column. It says here that "The tie with Michigan State was the greatest thrill associated with this columnist's career with The Observer."

"Darn right," said O'Connor.

Collins proceeded. "The field goal by an unheralded walk-on named Dutch Reagan was a near-miracle. If elections for student body president were held tomorrow, Dutch Reagan would probably win in the biggest landslide since student government's brief experiment with a monarchy in the early Seventies."

"You'd get my vote, Dutch," said Shenandoah Lee.

"Heck, I'd vote for you at least twice," said a player from Chicago.

Collins frowned.

"Hold on, guys. Summers isn't entirely convinced of our abilities. Listen to how the article ends: Yes, sports fans, a tie with the Spartans is a thrill. Unfortunately, based on past performance, the thrill may have to last us all year. It's really a shame the team had to peak so early in the season. Now, we may have nothing left to look forward to."

"PEAK SO EARLY IN THE SEASON?" Dutch said angrily. He was hot. "Anyone know there this Summers character lives?"

"Breen-Phillips. Why?"

"Dutch jumped up and strode toward the exit. "Because I'm going right over there to give him a piece of my mind!"

Collins called out to him. "Dutch! Wait! There's something you should know about Summers..."

Dutch was too enraged to hear. He was gone.

"Relax, Hart. He'll find out soon enough," said O'Connor.

"I'd sure like to be there when he comes face to face with the sports editor of The Observer."

Dutch Reagan covered the distance to Breen-Phillips Hall in seconds. The Hall was large enough to house about 230 students. He entered through the north doors which faced Farley Hall. A girl was coming out.

"Where does that idiot of a sports editor Summers live?" he demanded.

The girl was too startled to think. Without hesitation, she blurted out, "Room 305. Up the stairs, third floor, turn left."

Dutch took the stairs two at a time and flung open the double doors on the third floor landing. Halfway down the hall to his left, he found the door to Room 305*. He pounded on it so forcefully that one of the door's wooden panels fell in.

Moments later, the door swung open. A calm voice said, "May I help you?"

For once in his second life, George Gipp was speechless. Before him stood a girl in an ankle-length terrycloth robe. A towel was draped around her head. She had the most beautiful blue eyes he had ever seen.

"I'm sorry. I'm looking for somebody else. I'm very sorry to disturb you."

"Disturb? I just return from a shower, some hulk smashes in one of my door panels and you call it a slight disturbance?"

"I said I'm sorry. I was angry. Just moments ago I read what the sports editor of The Observer had to say about the Irish peaking so early in the season. When I find the jerk I'm going to let him know exactly what I think of him!"

"Oh, really?"

"The son of a gun doesn't deserve to be a sportswriter, let alone have a byline."

The blue eyes turned icy.

"Well, whoever you are, you just told 'him.' I'm Summers. Nicki Summers. I'm the sports editor of The Observer."

She slammed the door shut.

Dutch called through the open panel. "Wait..."

"Goodby!" The panel slammed back into place.

Great, just great, Dutch thought. He shuffled away.

He considered avoiding his friends for a few hours, but evidently they had anticipated the outcome of his surprise visit. He found them all waiting for him outside, leaning on the bike racks. He could tell they were all trying to keep from breaking up with laughter.

"I guess you really told 'him' off, right, Dutch?"

"Get an exclusive interview, Dutch?"

"Well, now you know one thing. Notre Dame may have the best looking college sports editor in the nation!" Collins said.

"How would I know? She was shrouded in terrycloth from her head to her toe. I'll get you for this, Hart!"

"Me? It's not my fault. I tried to stop you."

Reluctantly, Dutch surrendered.

"Besides," Hart continue, "Nicki's only the third female sports editor in the history of The Observer. How could you have been expected to know?"

Dutch thought, Indeed, how could I? When I was a student here the first time, there weren't even any females at Notre Dame.

Chapter Nine: THE TEN COMMANDMENTS OF NOTRE DAME

Tuesday's practice found the new chaplain, Father Rock, promoted to assistant-coach-for-a-day.

"Gather around, boys, gather around," said Coach Kelly at the start of practice Tuesday. "Today, we have something special for you. Our new chaplain, Father Rock, is going to make a special presentation. I want you to pay very close attention. Father..."

"Thanks, Joe. Well, boys, I guess you can call this session the gospel according to Father Rock. I'm going to give you some sound advice, some words to live by."

A dark blue Notre Dame Monogram blanket lay draped over an object on a small pedestal beside him.

"Boys, beneath this blanket are the secrets of winning football. What will be revealed to you here today will transform the Fighting Irish."

From between the clouds, a bright, shimmering shaft of light suddenly appeared, seemingly focused on the pedestal. Rock thought, "You hot dog! God always did have a flair for the dramatic. But I guess even He can be excused for being a showoff every now and then. Especially when you can do what He can do."

45

Gingerly, Father Rock removed the blanket.

Two stone tablets stood on the pedestal. There, etched in stone, were several lines written in English. They were numbered from one to ten.

The heading said: THE TEN COMMANDMENTS OF NOTRE DAME.

"Boys, I can't tell you where these came from. You wouldn't believe me if I did. Trust me. These came from a very knowledgeable source. Just know that if you memorize theses commandments, and practice them, you'll turn the Notre Dame football team into contenders for the national championship.

"For the benefit of those in the back, I'll read these out loud."

In a clear, compelling voice, Father Rock began reading.

"The first commandment. Thou shalt not tarnish the image of Notre Dame."

"The second commandment. Thou shalt always remember the importance of alumni contributions, and score touchdowns accordingly.

"The third commandment. Remember to always keep protected thy quarterback.

"The fourth commandment. Honor thy coach.

"The fifth commandment. Thou shalt not fumble.

"The sixth commandment. Thou shalt not get caught in the act of committing a needless penalty.

"The seventh commandment. Thou shalt not sell thy Notre Dame football tickets above their actual face value.

"The eighth commandment. Thou shalt not be a hot dog.

"The ninth commandment. Thou shalt not covet thy opponent's cheerleaders."

Father Rock paused.

"The last commandment is perhaps the greatest of all. Listen very carefully."

Authoritatively, Father Rock spoke.

"The tenth commandment. Thou shalt never lose to USC."

The student managers, always efficient, immediately began distributing copies of the ten commandments to the players.

"Insert these in the front of your playbooks, fellas. There will be a quiz tomorrow," said Coach Kelly.

Father Rock continued, "Keep these commandments and the Fighting Irish of Notre Dame will have a very good chance of winning a few games this year. Maybe quite a few."

Father Rock added, "Now, boys, if you break these commandments, you'll be held accountable to me. Coach Kelly has authorized me to dispense penance in the form of laps and push-ups. Are there any questions?"

O'Connor raised his hand.

"Ryan?"

"Father, which ones are mortal sins?"

"The first, fifth, seventh, and tenth. Especially the tenth."

47

"You mean the ninth one – the one about the cheerleaders – isn't a mortal sin?" O'Connor looked relieved.

"No, Ryan," Father Rock said, "It just wouldn't be fair. Whoever wrote the words, 'deliver us not into temptation,' had never seen the USC cheerleaders."

"So, what happens if a high-quality tight end like me breaks one of them?"

"Well, Ryan, when you meet Saint Peter at the Pearly Gates, I might suggest one thing."

"What's that, Father?"

"Show him your press clippings. And pray!"

Chapter Ten: VICTORY AT LAST

Joe Kelly nervously paced the sidelines. He was anxious for the Purdue game to begin.

Every home game posed unique challenges for the head football coach at the University of Notre Dame. Notre Dame Stadium was a place where men were measured against myths, a place where 59,075 assistant coaches* voiced immediate approval or displeasure after every key coaching decision. Notre Dame's loyal legions had one standing order: On fourth and one, go for it!

Few audiences were more knowledgeable about the game of football; none expected more from the young men who wore their colors.

Kelly knew the statistics*. He could quote the figures from Notre Dame's first 95 seasons with ease. The litany of success included an overall record of 634-181-40. A winning percentage of more than 75 percent. Eighty-four winning seasons. Eleven unbeaten, untied seasons – five of them under the legendary Knute Rockne. Ten more in which the Irish were unbeaten but suffered one or more ties. Twenty-five seasons in which only a single loss spoiled an otherwise unblemished season. During the first ninety-five years, only seven losing seasons had blemished the golden tradition of Notre Dame football.

The Class of 1950 had been especially privileged. They entered the university in the fall of 1946 and graduated in 1950. In all that time, they never saw a Notre Dame football team lose. Frank Leahy's "lads," as he called them, had compiled a record of 36-0-2.

He remembered attending a game in 1984 when Notre Dame welcomed the 1949 championship team home for a "silver anniversary celebration." The modern Irish team had trailed at halftime. After the 1949 team members had been introduced during halftime ceremonies, the student body chanted "Suit 'em up! Suit 'em up!" At the time, most of the men were in their fifties.

The alumni kept track of everything that impacted on the Notre Dame football program. Even Father Hesburgh, the world-renowned president of Notre Dame who had won more honorary degrees than Knute Rockne had won football games, wasn't immune. At one of Hesburgh's many retirement parties, the president of the Notre Dame Club of Chicago had publicly called attention to the Irish football team's winning percentage during the Hesburgh years.

And then there was the greatest legend of all, Knute Rockne himself. In 13 years as head coach at Notre Dame, from 1918 to 1930, Rockne's teams won 105 games, lost 12 and tied 5. No coach, past or present, pro or college, had ever surpassed his winning percentage in major competition. Rockne had five undefeated seasons, three national championships and a reasonable claim to a fourth. Who knows what Rockne might have accomplished if he hadn't been killed in a tragic plane crash at the age of 43?

Rockne had set a standard of excellence at Notre Dame that few coaches since have been able to match. Frank Leahy and Ara Parseghian had come very close.

Despite such pressures, Kelly remained optimistic about today's game. The Irish had enjoyed their best week of practice, he thought, since he had taken over as coach. The addition of Dutch Reagan and the new chaplain, Father Rock, had improved morale considerably. Reagan took some of the heat off Collins, who had up until now been the major offensive threat. When receivers failed him, Collins scrambled as well as any sophomore in the land. Collins said it was because he wished to live to be a junior.

The battle was joined. For three quarters, the Irish stood toe to toe with the Purdue Boilermakers, trading insults, injuries and the football. Both offenses generated yardage between the 30 yard lines, both defenses stiffened at the 30 and proved absolutely unyielding at the 20.

The hard-fought struggle took its toll. Exhausted players left the field or were carried off. Kelly began substituting fresh players early in the fourth quarter. Purdue's quarterback, a seasoned veteran, knew a green freshman when he saw one. He burned the unfortunate Kevin O'Hara for a touchdown, spoiling his debut as a cornerback.

Purdue's coach ordered his team to try the two point conversion. He didn't have much choice; he was running out of kickers. His placekicker had been eliminated early in the game, when Dutch Reagan charged through the line and literally sent a Purdue blocker flying into him. The 245-pound lineman-turned-missile had deflected a field goal attempt and saved Reagan a penalty for roughing the kicker.

The Purdue coach selected a reliable play that had worked to perfection all season long. His senior quarterback, the speediest in the Big Ten, faked a handoff to the fullback and darted toward the corner.

Not this time. Dutch Reagan met him at the one and introduced him to two unwary sideline photographers. The dazed quarterback recovered a Canon AE-1 in the end zone. A bewildered photographer tried to capture the moment on pigskin.

Notre Dame took command late in the fourth quarter. After a Purdue punt, Collins connected on four straight passes to Ryan O'Connor to move the Irish to Purdue's 38. Reagan got the ball and maneuvered through the Purdue defenders to the open field. The Purdue safety made a brilliant tackle at the six.

The Fighting Irish wouldn't be denied. Mike Samick, the center, exploded through the middle of the Purdue line. Collins practically walked in for the touchdown.

Tom Roberts' extra point gave the Irish their first lead in two years.

ND 7-Purdue 6.

The Boilermakers still had time to pull it out. They only needed a field goal to recapture the lead. With time running out, the Irish would have no time to retaliate.

Reagan sacked the Purdue quarterback three times in succession to prevent him from running or throwing out of bounds to stop the clock. He could tell time, too. And, he reasoned, if Purdue failed to score, the Irish wouldn't need to retaliate.

On fourth and 17, Purdue flooded the end zone with receivers. But Reagan's onslaught forced the quarterback to throw hard and in a hurry. The ball sailed harmlessly into the wall.

The clock was running down. The student section took up the chant:

TEN.

NINE.

EIGHT.

SEVEN.

SIX.

FIVE.

FOUR.

THREE.

TWO.

WON!!!

Students cascaded onto the playing field, rippling down from the northwest rows of stadium benches. A swirling flood of golden helmets swept Coach Kelly up to its crest. The Band of the Fighting Irish struck up the Notre Dame Victory March as 59,075 pairs of hands applauded.

In the lower levels of the press box, John Thornton fought for a telephone. This was news!

Notre Dame had won a football game!

Chapter Eleven: NICKI MAKES A PASS

The win over Purdue eased the pressures on everyone associated with the Fighting Irish. Late one lazy autumn afternoon, a few days after the game, Hart, Dutch, Ryan and Shenandoah were tossing a football around on the South Quad.

All four were dressed in cutoffs, various styles of Notre Dame T-shirts and blue-striped Adidas "Boston" athletic shoes.

Dutch was taking a turn at quarterback. He sent O'Connor deep. He was about to throw when a black-haired coed caught his eye. The ball he sent up became a wobbly, dying duck. It fell embarrassingly short of its target.

The girl couldn't resist commenting. "Is that the best you can do?"

Dutch grimaced. He turned to face her. Oh, no, not her. He recognized the unforgettable blue eyes instantly. It was Nicki Summers.

"I suppose you can do better."

"Try me."

"You're on."

Nicki set her books on the lawn. O'Connor had retrieved the football. He handed it to Nicki, who gripped it like a pro.

She whispered, "O'Connor. Hook and go."

Dutch defended on the play. O'Connor ran about ten yards. Nicki pump-faked and froze Dutch flatfooted in his tracks. O'Connor raced ten more yards. A determined Dutch quickly recovered and nearly closed the gap.

Nicki lofted a perfect spiral to O'Connor. The ball was right in his hands. He trotted across the sidewalk and spiked the ball.

When he came back, he handed Nicki the ball. "Even Hart rarely throws better than that. You get the game ball, Nicki."

Dutch stared at her in disbelief.

"Where did a girl learn to throw like that?"

Nicki gave him a charming, victorious smile. She flipped the ball to Dutch and gathered up her books.

"Five older brothers."

She walked away, whistling the Notre Dame Victory March.

Meanwhile, Father Rock had quickly become a fixture around the football offices. It seemed as if he had always been there. He became Coach Kelly's good friend and confidant. Often, he would stop by in the late hours with a fresh pot of coffee or snacks.

Kelly was amazed by Father Rock's knowledge of Notre Dame football lore, particularly the early days. It was almost as if Father Rock had seen it with his own eyes.

One evening he regaled Kelly with the story about when Notre Dame's famous Four Horsemen were the toast of the country, and the Seven Mules, who did the blocking, were starting to resent it. He said that Rockne had called a vote to determine which group contributed the most to the team's success. "Do you know what happened, Joe?"

"What, Father?"

"The line won. Seven to four."

At other times, the men discussed coaching philosophies. Once, Kelly spoke of the tremendous competition involved in recruiting the best high school athletes.

Father Rock said, "I think it would be a wonderful thing if a coach could just forget about all the high school and prep school wonders of the world and develop a team from among the students of the institution who came to his school because they liked it best and not because of an attractive offer made for athletic ability."

"You know, Father Rock. If I could find some boys like that, maybe we really could rebuild the Notre Dame program. But where do you find them?"

"Maybe they're right under your nose. After all, you did win a game last week. Let's review your roster. There's some real talent there already."

Father Rock continued. "First, there's Dutch Reagan. That's obvious.

"Then there's Hart Collins. He seems to be a natural leader, even if he is only a sophomore.

"Then there's that Irish kid from Cathedral Prep in Erie, Pennsylvania. He was an all-state tight end for the Ramblers, wasn't he? Ryan O'Connor. Collins to O'Connor. I'll bet you'll be hearing a lot of that before those two graduate."

"Anybody else?"

"Let's not forget that kid with the All American name. What is it? Shenandoah Lee?"

"You're right about that one, Father Rock. He's my most promising freshman, and a real speedster on defense. Did you know he was Indiana's 'Mr. Basketball' last year? He led the Muncie Central Bearcats to the state championship."

"That is impressive!"

"You know, those four kids probably could have played at any school in the country. I've always wondered why they settled for Notre Dame."

"Maybe that's your answer. Maybe they came here because they love the school and what it stands for. Maybe they're here for reasons more important than just football."

"You just might be right, Father Rock. But you know what? I think those four youngsters could be the core of a great Notre Dame team. A truly great Notre Dame team. And you know what else? Someday I'm going to set a goal for them that is truly worthy of their talents."

"Why not right now? As soon as you made the decision to stick with Dutch, Hart, Ryan and Shenandoah as your regular starters, the team really started to come together. There's some real momentum now. They're real high achievers, those four. So set a goal! To motivate them, you just need to point out the hill. They'll figure out how to take it!"

"Good idea, Father. Look out, Southern Cal, here come the Irish!"

Chapter Twelve: THE QUEST

It was a Friday night. Hart had arranged a blind date for Dutch with his girlfriend's roommate.

"I don't know about this, Hart. I've never been on a blind date before."

"What's the matter, Dutch, you're not scared, are you? You didn't seem to be afraid of Purdue's tackles last week."

"Tackles are one thing. Brunettes are something else."

"Trust me. You'll like her. She's Lauren's roommate so she can't be all bad." Collins had met Lauren Kennedy at last year's freshman mixer. It had been love at first sight. She was a lovely, tanned blonde from Connecticut. Many considered her the most attractive girl on campus.

Collins had arranged to meet the girls at the entrance to the Engineering Auditorium, which did double-duty as a lecture hall in the daytime and a movie theater at night. This week, the Student Union Movie Commission was staging a George Lucas revival, showing some of his old classics. Tonight's feature was The Empire Strikes Back.

Ryan O'Connor was joining them. He didn't have a date, but that wasn't unusual. He was forever faithful to his H.T.H., or 'home town honey," in Erie, a dark-eyed Italian girl named Linda.

Collins had been suppressing a smile all afternoon. Dutch was sure of it, but couldn't guess the reason. He knew the moment Lauren Kennedy arrived – with her roommate.

"Nicki," Lauren said, "I'd like you to meet Dutch Reagan. Dutch, this is Nicki Summers."

Nicki said, "This is a wonderful surprise. Dutch and I are practically old friends. We've met twice before."

Collins burst out laughing. "And Nicki won both rounds."

The group entered the auditorium and chose seats in the middle rows. For the next two hours, they were transported to another galaxy as Luke Skywalker, Han Solo and the other Star Wars heroes battled the forces of the Evil Empire.

Dutch seemed to enjoy the film most. He told Nicki he had never seen it before, which she thought was odd. Imagine someone who had never seen a Star Wars film!

After the movie, the party of five squeezed into Nicki's Camaro and drove to Denny's on U.S. 33, about ten minutes from campus. Many Notre Dame students chose to supplement their dining hall menu with an occasional meal off campus...just to be safe about good nutrition, vitamin requirements, and so forth.

Collins loved the movie. Every thoughtful, he tried to put it in broader perspective. "You know, my favorite character in the Star

Wars series has always been Han Solo, the pilot of the Millennium Falcon. No matter what happens, he always fights his way through. No matter what the odds..."

"Great or small?"

"Cut it out, Dutch, I'm trying to be serious. No matter what the odds, he always keeps trying, facing every challenge. Remember the scene when Han Solo and his friends are being chased by enemy spaceships and he decides to fly his ship, the Millennium Falcon, directly into an asteroid belt to avoid the laser blasts? The rest of them thought he was crazy. Remember how C3PO, the gold robot, told him the odds of successfully navigating a spaceship through an asteroid field were something like three thousand, seven hundred and twenty to one?"

His friends nodded.

Collins said, "What did he say?"

They knew.

They all said together, "Never tell me the odds!"

Collins paused.

"I know it's only a movie, but I wish we could instill a little of Han Solo's attitude into the team."

Nicki agreed. "You're right. I think the old Notre Dame teams had that kind of spirit, if you want to call it that. There always seemed to be a common thread through the great game stories. No matter how much time was left, the greatest Notre Dame teams played their hearts out until the final gun sounded."

"Especially when Joe Montana was quarterback!" Collins said. "Remember the Cotton Bowl game when Notre Dame trailed 34 to 12 with seven minutes and 37 seconds to play, and still won 35 to 34?"

For the next half hour, the group debated what had led to the downfall of the Notre Dame football program. There was general agreement that many factors had contributed to the decline: academic pressures, high admissions standards for student-athletes, and, of course, the routine scapegoat, coeducation. They all dismissed the "Samson and Delilah" theory advanced by some of the more cynical alumni who remained convinced that the downfall was inevitable as soon as the school went co-ed in the fall of 1972. The argument generally stated the players would be unable to concentrate on football with all those pretty girls on campus to distract them. Male students from those early days of co-education generally disputed that theory, and often supported their claim by producing visual evidence from the old Freshman Photo Directory, or "dog book," as it was more commonly known.

Finally, Collins said, "Sometime before we graduate, I want to win the national championship for Notre Dame. I don't really have any interest in pursuing professional football, but I sure would enjoy winning the national title for Notre Dame. I think that's a quest worth pursuing."

There was silence for a few moments while the others pondered his proposal.

Dutch broke the silence. "Like you said, Hart. Never tell me the odds. It's agreed. We win the national championship."

Nicki gave him an affectionate elbow. "Here, have another French fry, dreamer."

Around midnight, back on campus, Dutch walked Nicki back to Breen-Phillips. At the door, he said, "I really enjoyed this evening, Nicki."

"Me, too."

"Well, I guess I should be going now." He moved closer.

"I guess so. I'd invite you in, but it's almost pumpkin time. You know how strict our hall rector, Sister Sarah, is about parietals violations."

"Yeah. Well, Nicki..." He moved closer.

Nicki tilted her head slightly back.

Extending his arm, Dutch shook her hand vigorously.

"Well, goodnight, Nicki. Thanks again. Be seeing you." Then he rushed away.

Nicki folded her arms and sighed. She thought to herself, Typical Notre Dame male!

But he is cute. For a football player.

Chapter Thirteen: KELLY'S PROMISE

Coach Kelly's new strategy of starting the youngsters worked like a charm.

On October 1, the Fighting Irish exploded.

Dutch Reagan scored three touchdowns. Hart Collins added two aerial strikes to Ryan O'Connor. Shenandoah Lee returned a Stanford kickoff 86 yards for a touchdown.

The Irish beat Stanford 42-21 before a capacity crowd at Notre Dame Stadium.

The defense showed remarkable improvement. All of Stanford's scores had come from the air. The defensive front four literally forced Stanford to pass. The four freshmen had surrendered only sixty yards on the ground. One of them, Mike Ploszek, forced and recovered a fumble to set up Notre Dame's first score.

Notre Dame now owned a two game winning streak.

On October 8, the Irish traveled to Pittsburgh and raised their season record to 3-1-1.

The defense had another sterling performance, shutting out the Panthers for three quarters. This week the defensive secondary had greatly improved; they had put in extra practice time on interceptions. Pitt's only score came on a late fourth quarter field goal.

Fighting Irish 24-Pitt 3.

Monday morning, Notre Dame achieved national recognition: "also receiving votes" status in USA TODAY's "Top 25" college football rankings. Dutch Reagan was written up in a sidebar as the Midwest player of the week.

By Tuesday, Notre Dame's sports information director, Charlene Selleck, had her hands full honoring requests from sportswriters for press passes for Saturday's home game against No. 4 Miami. She made a mental note to order extra complimentary hot dogs, mustard and pickle relish for the press box.

When the team returned from Pittsburgh, they found their fellow students had rediscovered their enthusiasm for Notre Dame football. The Observer was filled with features about the Pitt game. The school paper's sportswriters had even picked Notre Dame as their consensus "upset special of the week." It was the first time in recent memory that The Observer had risked its journalistic integrity by predicting an Irish victory.

The defense was especially proud of a story entitled, "Our Lady's Tough Guys."

Suspense built throughout the week. Each afternoon, the marching band would step off from its quarters in Washington Hall. Their drum cadences echoed throughout the campus as they marched to the drill field.

"Football fever" had even infected the normally quiet classrooms of the Notre Dame Law School. The dean reinstated its previously recessed Friday lunchtime pep rallies...on a trial basis, of course.

The upcoming night game was to be nationally televised. ABC Sports had wanted to showcase the Miami Hurricanes, early contenders for the national title. The network decided to air the Notre Dame contest partly for nostalgic reasons, and planned a halftime feature on the Irish coaching legends.

Thursday morning, the Musco Lighting Co. trucks arrived from Muscatine, Iowa. They had illuminated every night game since the first one ever played under the lights at Notre Dame – a 23-17 win over Michigan on September 18, 1982.

Friday morning, the Goodyear blimp arrived to hover over the campus.

That evening, the marching band made its circuitous route through the Notre Dame campus, assuming its traditional role as the "pied piper" for the student body. Freshmen, sophomores, juniors and seniors stormed out of dorms and followed the band to Stepan Center.

Pep rallies were held at Stepan Center, a gold-colored geodesic dome situated on the northeast corner of campus. Inside, the concrete floor was smothered with human beings and Zahmbies, as the residents of Zahm Hall were more commonly known.

Human pyramids rose and fell in the festive atmosphere of Stepan Center. Genuine Irish flags – three bars of orange, white and green – waved madly about. Rolls of tissue paper crisscrossed the air, unrolling like so many jet streams in the upper reaches of the dome.

When the massive east doors parted to admit the band, the fans ignited. Drums thundered as brass and silver instruments turned up the volume with the Notre Dame Victory March. Many of the seniors had nearly forgotten the words, but with a little prompting from the freshmen they did fairly well. Everyone joined in the famous chorus:

> Cheer, cheer for old Notre Dame,
> Wake up the echoes cheering her name,
> Send a volley cheer on high,
> Shake down the thunder from the sky,
> What though the odds be great or small?
> Old Notre Dame will win over all.
> While her loyal sons are marching
> Onward to victory!

A group of co-eds had amended the final two lines to sing, "While her loyal sons and daughters march on to victory." In the noise, few heard them.

Onstage, the female cheerleaders pranced to the music under the protection of the male cheerleaders, who batted down any stray rolls of tissue paper entering their airspace.

The crowd let out a roar when Coach Kelly, Hart Collins, Dutch Reagan and the rest of the players and coaches bounded onto the platform.

When Joe Kelly stepped to the microphone, the crowd cheered. Despite his winless first season, he had at least won a measure of respect from the fans for losing with dignity. He had boosted his personal popularity among the students in April, when he and his assistant coaches entered a team in the springtime An Tostal Festival's Bookstore Basketball tournament. His team had soundly defeated the opponents who had taken to the court with a cruel but clever psychological ploy: each starter wore the jerseys of the five college football opponents who handed Coach Kelly his first five losses at Notre Dame. Kelly had personally scored the first 12 unanswered points.

Tonight, he was a real hero.

He finally settled the crowd and began to speak.

"When I first accepted the job as your head coach, I promised to do my best to bring the program back to the standards it enjoyed when I was a student at the university. It hasn't been easy, and we have a long way to go. At the beginning of this season, the players and coaches set a goal of winning at least three games. After the

71

opener with Michigan, we privately wondered whether we could even beat the Little Sisters of the Poor."

He paused until the laughter subsided.

"When Dutch Reagan kicked that field goal to tie Michigan State, we thought that maybe, just maybe, the luck of the Irish had reversed direction. Well, it has. Tonight, your Fighting Irish are 3-1-1!"

Cheers.

"Just before this pep rally...just before we came here to meet the greatest college football fans in the nation..."

More cheers. Notre Dame fans loved to applaud themselves.

"...we had a team dinner. Your Fighting Irish have set a new goal for this season...one we are sure you will all support. In the next few weeks we plan to ground the Air Force...sink Navy...convert Southern Methodist...cage the Nittany Lions..."

Kelly paused for a moment.

Would he dare say it?

"...and beat USC!!!"

Total bedlam.

"The Fighting Irish of Notre Dame...your Fighting Irish...plan to win every game the rest of this season. Your Fighting Irish will win a bid to a major bowl game. Your Fighting Irish will finish this season ranked among the top ten teams in the nation."

He stopped for just a slight moment.

"And we are going to start that victory march tomorrow by upsetting Miami for you in Notre Dame Stadium!"

It was almost too much for the win-starved Notre Dame student body. The band, recognizing a good cue when it heard one, instantly played the Victory March.

The crowd was beside itself. Coach Kelly had not only said it, he sounded like he meant it.

In turn, Collins, O'Connor and Lee took center stage and delivered rousing pep talks. O'Connor stole the show with his impression of Ronald Reagan doing George Gipp. An older Holy Cross priest was heard to say it rivaled Pat O'Brien's rendition of Knute Rockne.

Chapter Fourteen: GOD ONLY KNOWS

"Things are going rather well, Knute. Why do you need My help?" said the voice of God.

"Well, I know how much you enjoy a good practical joke, Lord," Rockne said, "I thought you'd want to be in on the fun."

"Hmmm. Well...it could be very funny. I'll do it!"

"Thanks, Lord."

Rockne caught the early morning rainbow back to Indiana. He was glad the planning session had gone well.

Everything goes a little better with God's help, he thought.

Chapter Fifteen: FOOTBALL SATURDAY

The Golden Dome blazed in sunlight against the backdrop of an unclouded, brilliant blue sky. Perfect weather for a football weekend.

This morning, northern Indiana had bedecked itself in its best autumn clothes. The trees were turning. Red, gold, and brown leaves blended well with the yellow-buff bricks of the buildings of Notre Dame. The oldest buildings were actually derived from the Indiana earth; rich marl deposits in St. Mary's Lake had yielded enough raw materials for the university to produce its own bricks and mortar.

Sedans, vans and recreational vehicles streamed from the exit ramps of the Indiana Toll Road. Uniformed South Bend police and Indiana state troopers kept traffic flowing smoothly as the sons and daughters of Notre Dame returned for a weekend visit.

On campus, various student groups commenced setting up outdoor grills, yellow sawhorses and blue tabletops at choice locations along the busiest walkways. Sales of hot dogs, hamburgers, bratwurst and soda pop were brisk. A favorite stop was the Knights of Columbus concession, renowned for its steak sandwiches.

The most popular place of all was the Hammes Notre Dame Bookstore. The first floor was alive with two colors – gold and blue.

The merchandise sparkled; the staff had started dusting off the inventory after the Pitt game and the job was now almost complete. T-shirts, caps, jackets, pennants, collectors' plates, coffee mugs and various and other souvenirs carried the words, Notre Dame, or bore the famous leprechaun, with his upraised fists, or the familiar "ND" monogram.

Books could be found on the second floor, if one was willing to climb the stairs.

Outside, bedsheet banners hung everywhere. One urged the Irish to weather the Hurricanes. One draped from a Sorin Hall turret offered an encouraging "GO IRISH!" Still another, hanging from the Administration Building, addressed a special audience: "DEAR ALUMNI, SEND MONEY." At first, the passing alumni thought it was a joke, then, realizing it hung from the window of the development office, knew better.

As morning turned to afternoon, the women of St. Mary's College, the nearby women's college, began wandering over in groups along the service road which led them past Holy Cross Hall and St. Mary's Lake to the center of campus.

The unofficial opening of the football game was the band's pre-game outdoor concert. An hour or so before kickoff, the band assembled on the front steps of the Administration Building. The show served as a final dress rehearsal for the halftime performance. Tonight's program was titled "An Irish Celebration," and an appreciative audience applauded performances of The Minstrel Boy, Foggy Dew, and The Garryowen.

Near the conclusion of the program, the band announcer intoned, "...and now we invite you to join in as the Band of the Fighting Irish plays the greatest of all fight songs: THE NOTRE DAME VICTORY MARCH!"

Immediately afterward, in the light of the setting sun, the faithful began the procession to Notre Dame Stadium.

Chapter Sixteen: MIRACLE AT NOTRE DAME

The unique traditions of Notre Dame were nowhere more evident than in the All American spectacle of its football games.

Night had fallen. Overhead, the sky was a deep blue-black. Inside the stadium it was as bright as day. The powerful Musco lights flooded the place with artificial sunshine, creating a kaleidoscopic panorama of brilliant colors and sharp contrasts.

The proud Notre Dame Band – the oldest university marching band in the United States – emerged from the north tunnel and dispersed its ranks in the end zone. The band members stood in attentive silence as the stadium announcer welcomed the faithful to Notre Dame Stadium.

A sharp whistle. The clatter of drumsticks. The rousing music of The Hike Song as the 225-member band began its famous hike-step routine to midfield.

The drum major sprinted to the fore. She was dressed in white from her shako to her boots, except for gold embroidery and epaulets.

Immediately after her came the members of the Irish Guard, photographers' delights in their scarlet coats and kilts woven of a specially-designed blue and gold plaid. Black shakos with orange plumes crowned their uniforms. The honor guard, comprised of male students who met a minimum height requirement of six feet, two inches, towered above the royal blue tam o'shanters worn by the musicians marching in their wake.

Every game started with a tribute to America. The band stood rigidly at mid-field and reverently played America the Beautiful. Meanwhile, an alumnus specially-chosen for the honor – this week an author from Chicago – carried a folded American flag diagonally from the 50 yard line to the northeast corner of the field. Members of the Irish Guard met him, snapped a salute, took custody of the Stars and Stripes and wheeled about to march to the flagpole.

There, the guardsmen respectfully unfolded, then raised and unfurled the red, white and blue flag while the band played the national anthem. There was no celebrity at a microphone to lead the singing. There was no need; the crowd sang on its own, without prompting.

One Chevrolet commercial later, the game was on.

The Irish kicked off.

The specialty team hurtled downfield and drove the Miami return man into the turf at the 12 yard line.

"Our Lady's Tough Guys" stopped the first attempt at the line of scrimmage.

On Miami's second play, the fullback was nailed at the 10.

On the third, the Hurricane quarterback was sacked at the five.

Definitely a punting situation.

The Hurricane punting unit moved into position. Shenandoah Lee and Dutch Reagan were back for the Irish.

On the Irish bench, Father Rock removed his hat and made the Sign of the Cross. It was the agreed upon signal.

"Do your stuff, Lord," he whispered.

The toe of the Hurricane kicker met the ball as thunder rolled across the sky. The football hit the ground at the 50 yard line and began a series of freak bounces that even a Detroit Tigers shortstop couldn't have fielded.

Reagan retreated, moving quickly to overtake the football. His fingertips touched the ball as another thunderclap boomed overhead.

Out of thin air, a lightning bolt flashed directly above Notre Dame Stadium. Splitting into four branches, the lightning arced over the stadium walls and struck Musco Lighting Co.'s electrical equipment. Sparks flew. Electricity sizzled.

Onrushing Hurricanes had Reagan in their eyes when the Musco lights went out, plunging the field into darkness.

It was pitch black! For eight long seconds, total darkness enveloped the stadium. Then the lights flickered, grew bright and finally bathed the stadium in light once more.

Dutch Reagan was at the Miami three! His golden helmet flashed across the goal line!

The field behind him was littered with bodies. In desperation, the Miami defenders had tackled the sounds of footsteps. As a result, they had mostly tackled each other.

Confusion reigned supreme. The ABC announcers were so confounded that when the referee called an official timeout, they forgot to cut to a commercial. The officials huddled at the Miami sideline. The Hurricane coach offered them his counsel at the top of his voice.

There were no penalty flags on the field. "You can't call what you can't see," one official later told a sportswriter. No whistles had blown, either.

The head referee raised his arms straight up from his shoulders. Touchdown, Notre Dame.

The stadium erupted as the Notre Dame family woke up the echoes, all of Indiana and most of Illinois and Michigan.

The victory march had begun in earnest.

With national television as a showcase, the Fighting Irish presented a dazzling array of football prowess that delighted their admirers and stunned their opponents.

By the middle of the third quarter, Dutch Reagan had racked up 148 yards rushing, and in a bit of razzle-dazzle had launched a scoring pass to Hart Collins for the fifth Irish touchdown.

Up in the press box, even John Thornton was at a loss for words. Could this really be the Fighting Irish of Notre Dame, only a few weeks ago the laughingstocks of college football?

In his mind, he summoned up the vocabulary of winners. He conjured up images of Notre Dame legends of seasons past. He hit upon the famous paragraph written in 1924 by Grantland Rice, one of the most famous sportswriters of all time. Rice's words had immortalized another Notre Dame backfield:

"Outlined against a blue-gray October sky the Four Horsemen rode again. In dramatic lore they are known as famine, pestilence, destruction and death. These are only aliases. Their real names are: Stuhldreher, Miller, Crowley and Layden. They formed the crest of the South Bend cyclone before which another fighting Army team was swept over the precipice at the Polo Grounds this afternoon as 55,000 spectators peered down upon the bewildering panorama spread out upon the green plain below."

Rice's words alone might have been enough to catapult the four players to glory. Their immortality was assured when an enterprising student publicist named George Strickler led four horses to the practice field a few days later. All four mounted horses for the first time in their lives and became forever known as the Four Horsemen of Notre Dame.

Thornton envied Rice's skill and fame. He pounded the typewriter's keys furiously. He was going to write the most famous story of his career.

On the field, the Irish added two more touchdowns in the final quarter. The final score was Notre Dame 56-Miami 0.

As he headed to the locker room, Father Rock looked up and gave a smile and a wink to a passing cloud.

Chapter Seventeen: THE GIPPER'S GHOST

By noon Sunday, a hastily-painted bedsheet banner draped above the entrance to Dutch Reagan's dormitory. It said, "Sorin Hall – Home of the Gipper's Ghost."

When Dutch saw it, he thought, if they only knew!

John Thornton's column was being pasted into scrapbooks all over campus. Father Sinon, the hall rector, had even arranged for an enlarged Photostat to be made and tacked onto Dutch's door.

Headlined GIPPER'S GHOST HAUNTS MIAMI, the story read as follows:

"The spirit of Notre Dame turned out the lights on Miami last night in a terrifying display of skill and speed. The Fighting Irish played as if possessed, as if the ghosts of the legends of Notre Dame had arisen to reclaim their lost heritage of victory. If so, then there can be little doubt that the Gipper's ghost lived in the heart of Dutch Reagan, who disappeared the first time he held the ball and reappeared at the goal line for Notre Dame's first touchdown of the game.

"Invisible in the blackness of a dark October night, the Gipper's Ghost led the reincarnation of the Fighting Irish of Notre Dame. Let future opponents beware: the House that Rockne Built is haunted indeed. In one eerie moment when an act of God shook down the thunder from the Indiana sky, a bolt of lightning woke up the echoes of Notre Dame's past and served notice that the slumbering giant of college football has been reborn."

The remainder of the story summarized the scoring details. A sidebar reported that Musco Lighting's public relations people were at a loss to explain the momentary blackout. The Miami coach had only three words to explain it. "Deus ex machina." An act of God.

At the team dinner Monday evening, the players were not only ready to believe in ghosts, they had started to believe in miracles. More importantly, they were starting to believe in themselves. Maybe their dream of finishing in the "Top Ten" could come true. But first, they had to deal with Air Force.

The Falcons from Colorado Springs had emerged as the football powerhouse of America's military academies. In 1984, they had become the first service academy ever to defeat Notre Dame three seasons in a row. Anyone who thought the Air Force lacked infantry never faced their rushing attack.

On the third weekend in October, the Irish ruled the skies, making six interceptions.

Irish 42-Air Force 0.

The next week the Irish ranked in the top 15 in all of the major college football polls.

On the final weekend of October, Collins fired salvo after salvo into Navy's secondary. Shenandoah Lee picked off two passes for touchdowns. The Midshipmen avoided being the third straight Irish shutout victim by kicking a last minute field goal. Final score: Notre Dame 38-Navy 3.

The Irish were on a roll. After their sixth straight victory, the pollsters could no longer ignore Notre Dame. Including the disastrous opening day loss to Michigan, the Irish had outscored their opponents 230 to 92. They were averaging more than 400 yards total offense. The defense had not surrendered a touchdown in 17 consecutive quarters. Their record was 6-1-1.

Associated Press ranked the Irish No. 6, United Press International No. 5, and USA TODAY had moved them up to No. 4.

Scouts from five major and minor bowls were on hand to watch Notre Dame defeat Southern Methodist 48-0.

Seven straight victories. In the past five games, Notre Dame had put 208 points on the scoreboard to their opponents' six.

Maybe this year the Fighting Irish wouldn't have to spend New Year's Day watching television at home.

Unless...

Chapter Eighteen: WOMAN'S INTUITION

Something had happened earlier in the week that might have an unfortunate impact on Notre Dame's bowl chances.

"Dutch, your hair is getting a little long, don't you think?" Nicki had asked at breakfast the past Tuesday morning. "Why don't you let me give you a haircut?"

"After what happened to Samson, forget it."

"Well, at least let me make you an appointment at the university barber shop."

"Nicki..."

"You do like me, don't you?"

"Of course, I do."

"Good. I'll make an appointment for 10:00 a.m."

Dutch and Nicki had become a steady item. The pair had made a habit of starting the day together ever since Dutch discovered she routinely rose for an early breakfast in "A" line of the North Dining Hall. Dutch, whom his roommate Collins said never climbed out of bed until at least 10 o'clock before his first date with Nicki, had reformed completely.

He was up, showered and shaved by seven, just so he could be near Nicki.

After breakfast, the two often took a brisk stroll around one of the lakes before Nicki's eight o'clock class. It was during Tuesday morning's walk that her suspicions were first aroused.

Although Nicki adored Dutch Reagan, certain things about him puzzled her. Although he had a fascination with early 20th century history, his grasp of more recent events was minimal. He had an almost childlike enthusiasm for such everyday, routine items as personal computers and videocassette recorders. And he used the oddest language at times. Quaint, almost antiquated. And there was another thing. She had often wondered why someone with such remarkable athletic gifts had never been "discovered" in high school. Surely, at least one of Notre Dame's alumni scattered throughout the country would have dropped a line about him to the athletic department.

Anyway, Dutch had been amusing her by retelling some of his favorite anecdotes about his football-playing experiences, when he said something that haunted her.

Dutch had said, "Well, here Norm Barry and I were having a little friendly competition to see who could score the first touchdown against Valparaiso..."

Norm Barry. That's odd, Nicki had thought. As sports editor, I know almost every player on the team. I don't remember a Norm Barry.

Later that day, from her desk in The Observer office, she called the Sports Information Department for background information about Dutch for a profile she was writing for the newspaper. It struck her as odd how little information Charlene Selleck had about Dutch. Charlene usually had every detail at her fingertips. If a Notre Dame football player had thrown his first football at age two, Charlene would know about it, and publicize it.

Curious.

Nicki told herself, you're a sportswriter, not an investigative reporter. More than that, Dutch is your friend. More than that...Dutch may be...more than that.

Norm Barry...

She reached into her file drawer and pulled out her reference copy of the annual Notre Dame Football Guide. She scanned this year's team roster. No Norm Barry listed.

Something – woman's intuition perhaps – compelled her to turn to the all-time roster which indexed the names of every football player who had earned a Notre Dame Monogram. Interesting. There were three Norm Barrys listed: one around 1920, another around 1940, and another around 1970. She thought, Wouldn't it be something if all these guys were related?

She tried to recall Dutch's exact words: "Well, here Norm Barry and I were having a little friendly competition to see who could score the first touchdown against Valparaiso..."

Valparaiso!

She began frantically searching past schedules, looking for...who knows?

Then she found an even bigger clue.

Notre Dame hadn't played a football game against Valparaiso since the year 1920.

Chapter Nineteen: AN INVITATION

Today's the day, Father Romano!" said an exuberant "Wild Bill" Fallon.

Fallon could hardly contain his excitement. He had lived and breathed Notre Dame from the very first day he was born. "Wild Bill" often said he was quite proud of the fact that he shared his birthday, March 4, with the legendary Knute Rockne.

"You are going to accept a bowl bid, aren't you, Father?" Fallon said, covering all the bases. Fallon, Charlene Selleck and Father Martin Cockrell had assembled in the university president's office. They didn't want to take a chance on missing a telephone call from a bowl committee. Any bowl committee.

"Of course, Bill. The only question is, which one? We might receive invitations from the Cotton, Orange and Sugar Bowl committees."

"True. The Orange Bowl Committee attended last week's game," said Father Cockrell. "A spokesman for their committee told me the Irish were receiving serious consideration. However, he said they prefer to get Penn State, and since they're on our schedule already, we probably won't get invited if Penn State accepts."

"Frankly, I'd almost prefer somewhere else. I'm not sure Notre Dame will be very welcome in Miami after what happened earlier in the season," Fallon said.

"Well, that seems to leave the Sugar and Cotton Bowls," said Father Romano. "Truthfully, I think the alumni would even welcome a trip to the Cherry Bowl in the Pontiac Silverdome."

The men engaged in excited conversation for the next several minutes, reviewing the day's games and speculating about probable bowl matchups.

The telephone rang. The conversation stopped immediately.

Father Romano let the phone ring twice, then he picked up the handset. He listened for some time, then spoke into the phone, "Yes, sir. Thank you very much for your kind invitation. The University of Notre Dame football team would be very proud to participate in the Sugar Bowl Classic."

He listened for a minute, then politely said goodby.

"Did he say who'll we'll play?" asked Charlene Selleck. The sports information director was seated at Father Romano's word processor and had already begun keyboarding a news release.

"No. They expect an answer shortly from their other choice. He said it will be announced on ABC's next sports update."

Fallon turned on the television set while Father Romano dialed a phone number.

"Who are you calling? The student ombudsman service?" joked Father Cockrell.

"No. But university presidents are allowed to wake up a few echoes now and then, too, aren't they?"

Minutes later, per Father Romano's instructions, the ringing of the bells of the Sacred Heart Church carillon coincided with the sports report.

The announcer intoned, "It's been a great day for the Fighting Irish. First, the Irish corralled the Mustangs of SMU by shutting them out 48 to 0. Dutch Reagan – the Gipper's Ghost – scored his seventeenth touchdown of the season."

He paused while the graphics changed to show a sugar bowl.

"Second, moments ago University of Notre Dame officials accepted a bid to the Sugar Bowl Classic to be played in the Superdome in New Orleans. The Irish opponent will be the Tigers of Louisiana State University."

"The LSU Tigers!" Fallon exclaimed.

A fairy tale season was falling into place. The Irish were certain to move up in the polls again this week. Once again, the students could cautiously begin kidding their friends and relatives that Notre Dame played in the "Top Ten" conference.

Only three obstacles remained. No. 2 Penn State. No. 1 USC. And now, No. 3 LSU.

And perhaps, one very suspicious female sportswriter.

Chapter Twenty: NICKI'S DISCOVERY

It happened on Tuesday.

Nicki had been researching a term paper for her Feature Writing class on the topic of the Golden Age of Sports. The Memorial Library housed an extensive International Sports and Games collection, a perfect place to research the subject.

As she leafed carefully through the old books and research materials, she naturally gave special attention to references to Notre Dame, Knute Rockne and the other legends of Fighting Irish history. But she wasn't prepared for the shock when she opened a manila folder marked "George Gipp." The eyes staring at her from the photograph were hauntingly familiar.

In the wink of an eye, all the clues came together.

Norm Barry. Valparaiso. 1920.

"Oh, my God. I know who he is."

The confrontation came the next morning. After breakfast, Dutch and Nicki took their usual stroll around the lake. They were nearly halfway around it when Nicki grew strangely silent. Dutch wondered why.

She broke the quiet.

"Do you think we'll win on Saturday, George?"

"Are you kidding? We'll do just great. Hart's been very sharp in practice and..." He stopped. "One unguarded moment," he thought. "What did you call me?"

"You're George Gipp, aren't you? I don't know how or why, and God knows this season has been enough to make an Irish Catholic believe in miracles, but you are George Gipp, aren't you? Please tell me the truth."

Dutch had promised Nicki he would never lie to her. He couldn't do it now.

"Yes, Nicki. It's true."

"George...Dutch...what do I call you now...what do I do...this is possibly the biggest story of my life...I should write this up for The Observer...the world should know...an angel of God saves the Notre Dame football team singlehandedly..."

In a rare moment of modesty, Dutch said, "That's not quite accurate. God knows I'm no angel, and I'm not acting alone..." He wished he hadn't said that.

"There are MORE of you? Who else?"

"Rock's here, too."

Slowly, it dawned on her who "Rock" was.

"You mean Knute Rockne. THE Knute Rockne?"

I must be losing my mind, she thought.

She asked. Which one of my friends is he? No, don't tell me. Let me guess. Hart? No. Shenandoah? No. Please don't tell me it's Lauren."

"None of the above, Nicki. He's Father Rock, the team chaplain. God thought that would make a great cover for him."

"This isn't happening," Nicki thought.

"In the last three minutes, you've told me that you're George Gipp, that Knute Rockne is alive and well and wearing a Roman collar, and that you talk to God on a regular basis!"

"Doesn't everybody?"

"That's beside the point. Good Lord!"

"Nicki, I can't let you write that story. It might upset God's plan. This is bigger than both of us. And besides, no one will believe you."

Just then, the full implications hit Nicki. She burst into tears.

"Now what's wrong?"

"Everything, Dutch! My whole life. Do you know what you have really told me?"

"What?"

"You've just told me I've fallen in love with a ghost. All the men available on the campus of the University of Notre Dame and I fall in love with 'The Gipper's Ghost.' Only, you really are a ghost!"

She ran away. She called over her shoulder, "I don't think I can see you anymore. Ever."

Tears filled her eyes as she ran back to Breen-Phillips. She entered her room, locked the door and hurled herself onto her bed, weeping bitterly.

A dozen peach-colored roses were delivered to her room two hours later. The note was from Dutch.

"Nicki," the note began, "I'm very sorry this happened. The truth is, I love you, too. Always will. Maybe someday we can be together again. Dutch."

She cried for two more hours.

Later, she was able to compose herself. She went to her office at The Observer, on the third floor of LaFortune Student Center.

She didn't write the story. She did ask for a favor from the ad manager.

The next day, Dutch Reagan discovered a message in the "Personals" column of The Observer classifieds:

GEORGE: YOUR SECRET IS SAFE WITH ME. I'LL ALWAYS REMEMBER YOU.

Chapter Twenty-One: RESTORING THE LUSTRE

A capacity crowd assembled in Penn State's stadium to witness the showdown between the No. 2 ranked Nittany Lions and the resurrected 8-1-1 Fighting Irish.

Both teams were bowl bound. Penn State would face the Ohio State Buckeyes in the Orange Bowl and Notre Dame the undefeated LSU Tigers in the Sugar Bowl. The outcome of today's game would figure in the determination of the mythical national champion.

The Nittany Lions emerged from the tunnel first. The Irish followed.

"Our Lady's Tough Guys" set the tone with an epic defensive effort which held the Nittany Lions without a single yard gained in the first quarter.

Hart Collins led a 64 yard drive in seven plays to score with 2:32 remaining in the first quarter. The kick failed.

ND 6-Penn State 0.

Halfway through the second quarter, Penn State scored on a six yard run. The extra point was good.

Penn State 7-ND 6.

Dutch Reagan returned the kickoff 87 yards for a touchdown. Collins passed to him for the two-point conversion.

ND 14-Penn State 7.

Only 39 seconds remained in the first half when Penn State's kicker connected on a field goal.

ND 14-Penn State 10.

In the locker room, Joe Kelly spoke to his team. "In the first half, you showed them you could play with one of the best teams in the country. In the second half, show them you are the nation's best."

The brave words suffered at the start of the second half. Penn State marched 93 yards and took the lead on a five yard scoring plunge by Harris Berg.

Penn State 17-ND 14.

The Fighting Irish fought their way past midfield. A long field goal attempt fell short.

Mike Ploszek forced a fumble at the Penn State 12 with 2:30 remaining in the third quarter. Collins scrambled 12 yards on the next play. Roberts' kick was good.

ND 21-Penn State 17.

Penn State breakaway! Touchdown!

The kick for the point after was smothered by a wall of Notre Dame linemen.

Penn State 23-ND 17.

In the offensive huddle, Collins had few words. "Gentlemen, the time is now."

The Fighting Irish marched 79 yards on 11 plays. The Nittany Lions scratched and clawed and finally stopped them at the three...momentarily. The next play was a touchdown for Hart Collins. Tom Roberts strode in and drilled the extra point through the uprights with 4:26 remaining.

ND 24-Penn State 23.

Once again, the Notre Dame defense subdued the Lions. Penn State was forced to punt. But what a punt! 69 yards! The ball was downed at the Notre Dame one.

A fumble might be recovered by Penn State. An interception in this area might be turned into a score for the opponents. A safety would give the Nittany Lions two points and certain victory.

Collins kept the ball twice and burrowed his way to the five. On third and six, he fired to Ryan O'Connor at the 37. O'Connor brought it down and hit the turf.

The clock whirred off the remaining seconds.

Notre Dame's jubilant celebration was short-lived. There, on the goal line, lay the motionless form of Dutch Reagan.

Dutch had been assigned to block Killer Kubinski, Penn State's 275 pound middle linebacker. There had been a major collision. The full weight of an unconscious Killer Kubinski had collapsed on Dutch Reagan's right leg.

The Gipper's Ghost had proved all too human. His leg was broken.

Chapter Twenty-Two: OUT FOR THE SEASON

"What's going on, Rock?" Dutch had sought out Rockne as soon as he was released from the hospital. He was wearing a full leg cast.

"Where'd you get the crutches, Dutch?" Father Rock asked.

"Gift from an admirer. Stop evading the question. You know as well as I do that it's impossible for a guardian angel to get a broken leg unless it's part of the plan. What's going on? I mean, after today, we're sure to be ranked third in the country. Next week, we play Southern Cal. I don't understand, Rock. The team needs me!"

"We've done all we were supposed to do, George. We've shown them the way. Breaking your leg was the most convincing method God could think of to take you out for the rest of the season without arousing undue suspicion," Rockne said.

"Without me, the Fighting Irish don't have a ghost of a chance against the Trojans. Rock, you told us breaking the tenth commandment is a mortal sin. Surely you don't want great guys like Joe and Hart roasting for eternity in Hell just because I got a broken leg and consequently they lost to USC! There has to be something you can do!"

"If the Fighting Irish are going to win the national championship, they're going to have to win it on their own. It's God's will, George," said Rock.

"Then, there's nothing you can do?"

"Well, He did say I could make one of my patented locker room speeches. But only if I have to. Only if it's an emergency."

"Does this mean I'll be heading back to Purgatory soon?"

"It means nothing of the sort. That kickoff you returned for a touchdown against Penn State evened up your account in the Permanent Record. You're going to Heaven, my boy!"

Dutch looked sad. "It might as well be Purgatory."

Rock guessed the reason. "It's Nicki, isn't it?"

"Yeah. I was hoping to patch things up before we left. Now I guess I'll never get the chance."

Chapter Twenty-Three: WHAT THOUGH THE ODDS

At the team meeting Monday night, Dutch Reagan stood supported by crutches when he told his teammates to play their best against USC on Saturday. His words seemed to help the Irish maintain a hard-working attitude at practice.

Coach Kelly tried a few tricks to help ease the tension. He hired a student to wear a Trojan costume and charge onto the playing field aboard a great white stallion on Tuesday afternoon.

Speculation about the game was at a fever pitch. Many sportswriters predicted the Irish' miracle season would come to an abrupt end on Saturday. By upsetting Penn State, the Irish had helped USC solidify its No. 1 ranking. The Irish had moved up to No. 3, just a few votes behind LSU.

Yet, conventional wisdom said, "No Dutch Reagan, no national championship."

And just when things couldn't get any worse, they got worse.

On Wednesday, the new issue of Sports Illustrated hit the newsstands. Notre Dame was featured on the cover!

The most dreaded curse in college football had struck the Fighting Irish. The Sports Illustrated jinx!

"No! It can't be."

"Not that! Anything but that!"

"Not before our last home game!" wailed a senior.

The cries of the wounded were heard from Pangborn Hall to Flanner Tower.

Oh, how the mighty had fallen once visited by the Sports Illustrated jinx! How many kings of sport had been dethroned by the terrible swift lens of Sports Illustrated's photographers!

Local legend told how trusty Tom Clements, one of Notre Dame's bravest quarterbacks, had been on the cover of the magazine once, in 1974. The story said he was "heir to a great tradition." The writer had meant a great tradition of Notre Dame quarterbacks which included Johnny Lujack, Paul Hornung and Joe Theismann. The students had known better, and feared the worst. Within days, the Irish – the defending national champions – were upset by the spoilermakers of Purdue.

Now, here it was again. The jinx.

Dutch Reagan was shown on the cover, in gold helmet and white road uniform, streaking to a touchdown against Southern Methodist. The headline said: THE GIPPER'S GHOST? NOTRE DAME'S HOLY TERROR!

Wasn't it bad enough that the Trojans were ranked No. 1 and had yet to suffer defeat? Dutch missing. And now this. No wonder Dutch Reagan's leg was broken. Sports Illustrated's presses probably started rolling Saturday afternoon and, SNAP!, Dutch Reagan is out for the season.

Coach Kelly could tell his players were jittery just by watching the practice sessions the rest of the week.

The mood was somber in "F" line of the North Dining Hall Thursday night after practice. The players barely touched their steaks.

"The Trojans have remained unbeaten for 34 consecutive games," said Ryan O'Connor. "Even with Dutch, we'd have to play the best game of our lives to beat them."

"That's right," said Shenandoah Lee. "This year's tailback, 'Rocket' Crockett, has made the fabled USC power sweep virtually unstoppable. And their All American linebacker, "Raging Bull" Karlson, is a devil in disguise on defense. The newspapers call him the Quarterback Cruncher."

Collins was quiet. He was thinking about the five quarterback sacks the Trojan defensive unit, led by "Raging Bull" Karlson, had averaged per game this season.

It was a glum, discouraged Notre Dame team that shuffled out the door of the dining hall a few minutes later. They turned south on the sidewalk. At the head of the group, Collins halted – and pointed at Farley Hall.

"In spite of anything opponents can do they can never be Notre Dame. They can never represent her glory, only try to steal some. They can't upset her traditions or her spirit, only attack them. They can win on the football field but not in our hearts, for they can never be NOTRE DAME: her people, her traditions, her football, her life."

From every dormitory on the North Quad – Farley, Breen-Phillips, Cavanaugh, Zahm, Keenan and Stanford – hung banners of every size and description. GO IRISH. SACK TROY. WIN ONE FOR THE GIPPER.

Suddenly, a whistle-blast pierced the air. A clatter of drumsticks. From a hidden position behind Farley and Breen-Phillips, the Band of the Fighting Irish marched into the open. And then from behind the other buildings appeared the students of Notre Dame.

The entire student body sang the Notre Dame Victory March from beginning to end:

Rally sons of Notre Dame:
Sing her glory and sound her fame.
Raise her Gold and Blue
And cheer with voices true:
Rah, rah for Notre Dame.
We will fight in every game.
Strong of heart and true to her name
We will ne'er forget her
And will cheer her ever
Loyal to Notre Dame.

Cheer, cheer for old Notre Dame,
Wake up the echoes cheering her name,

Send a volley cheer on high,

Shake down the thunder from the sky,

What though the odds be great or small?

Old Notre Dame will win over all,

While her loyal sons are marching

Onward to victory!

For the next half hour, various spokesmen addressed the team, including "Wild Bill" Fallon and Father Cockrell. Finally, Father Patrick Romano, the president of Notre Dame, approached the microphone.

"It's been a long time since this little American school with the French name and the Irish nickname has had a football team whose record matched this university's commitment to excellence. But you young men have made us proud, winning eight games in a row and conducting yourselves with as much grace in victory as you had shown in defeat. We wish you success on Saturday, but want you to know that we will be proud of you, whether you win or whether you lose, because you are part of the Notre Dame family!"

Then, Father Romano himself led the students in singing the alma mater, Notre Dame, Our Mother.

In the soft light reflected by the Golden Dome, visible between Zahm and Cavanaugh Halls, the student body rekindled the spirit of Notre Dame.

Chapter Twenty-Four: ND'S GREATEST RIVAL

The greatest college football rivalry of them all matched Notre Dame with USC. The Fighting Irish and the Trojans had shared the most memorable series in college football.

The long and storied tradition had assumed epic proportions. Many games and players had become the stuff of legends; some of the games even had names of their own.

The first contest was held in 1926. Notre Dame won 13-12.

The second one was in 1927 at Soldier Field in Chicago, where a crowd of 120,000 watched the Irish win 7-6.

Southern Cal got its turn in 1928, winning 27-14.

In 1929, Notre Dame won 13-12. In 1930, Rockne's last coaching victory came at Southern Cal. The Irish won 27-0.

"The Game" often figured in the national championship. In 1964, Ara Parseghian's first year at Notre Dame, a storybook team – which had lost seven games the year before – came within 1:33 of winning the national championship. What stopped them? A fourth quarter touchdown by the Trojans of Southern Cal. USC 20-ND 17.

The next year, the Irish won the "Remember" game. Banners hung around campus the preceding week, including one on top of the Golden Dome itself, said just one word: REMEMBER. Southern Cal entered Notre Dame Stadium undefeated and departed with a loss. Notre Dame 28-USC 7.

In 1966, the Irish clinched a national championship with a 51-0 conquest. According to legend but not verifiable fact, USC coach John McKay vowed he would never again lose to a Notre Dame team. Legend or not, he almost didn't.

The teams tied 21-21 in 1968. That day the Irish held a Trojan senior, O.J. Simpson, to his all time low, 55 yards on 21 carries.

Southern Cal spoiled another perfect season in 1970. The Irish were 9-0. USC won 38-28. Joe Theismann and the team took out their frustrations on a Texas team that had won 30 consecutive games by beating them in the Cotton Bowl 24-11.

Anthony Davis scored six touchdowns for USC in 1972. He started by taking the opening kickoff 97 yards for the first of six touchdowns. He performed a little dance in the end zone after all six. USC 45-ND 23.

By the time the Trojans visited Notre Dame the next autumn, they had gone 23 games without a loss. Hundreds of copies of a photograph of Anthony Davis – on his knees in the end zone – literally wallpapered the campus. The Observer ran one full page which featured the photo six times!

This day would be different.

Anthony Davis was held to 55 yards as the Irish outrushed the Trojans 316 to 68. Eric Penick's electrifying 85 yard gallop keyed the first Notre Dame victory since 1966. The final score was Notre Dame 23-USC 14. After the game, someone suggested that perhaps Penick should have completed his run by sliding on his knees in the USC end zone. Penick sharply responded, "I'm no hot dog. This is Notre Dame."

The game propelled Notre Dame toward a national championship. Ara's Irish upset No. 1 Alabama in the Sugar Bowl to finish the season 11-0.

Southern Cal got even the next year, and how! Notre Dame led 24-6 at the half. USC enjoyed the next 17 minutes by nonchalantly scoring 49 unanswered points. USC 55-ND 24.

Who could forget Dan Devine's "Green Jersey" game of 1977? The Irish warmed up in blue, went back to the locker room and returned wearin' the green to conquer the favored Trojans 49-19. Notre Dame went on to beat No. 1 ranked Texas in the Cotton Bowl. The Irish were voted national champions.

In 1984, Gerry Faust achieved something no Irish coach had accomplished since Ara Parseghian in 1966. In a muddy battle, Faust's Irish defeated USC in the Los Angeles Coliseum.

Last year had been a disaster for Notre Dame. The only bright point for the Irish had been the discovery of Hart Collins. Kelly put the fourth-string freshman in at the start of the fourth quarter. Collins scored a touchdown on his first play as a Notre Dame quarterback.

As far as the Irish were concerned, however, the overall memory of that 63-6 defeat was still a fresh wound.

Chapter Twenty-Five: THE SPIRIT OF NOTRE DAME

USC's head football coach, Troy Achilles, was shrewd enough to capitalize on any situation. When the USC offense assumed the set position on the first down of the game, the Irish defense was flabbergasted. Varnished and lacquered onto the top of every blood-red helmet facing them was the cover of Sports Illustrated. Achilles had bought up every unsold copy he could find and assigned his student managers the job of affixing the covers to the Trojan helmets.

USC scored first.

USC scored second.

USC scored third.

USC scored fourth.

Mercifully, the half ended. A deflated Notre Dame team trailed 24-0. The 59,075 assistant coaches of Notre Dame Stadium had fallen silent as their dream season collapsed before their eyes.

In the locker room, Coach Kelly was almost stricken dumb. There were few words. He looked around the room, surveying the damage. The team had limped into the locker room, carrying its wounded. The Trojans hadn't taken any prisoners...at least, not yet.

No one was talking. Players and coaches alike stared glumly at the floor.

Kelly summoned the courage to speak.

"Gentlemen, I don't know where to begin..."

"Well, I do!"

A startled team and their head coach turned toward the voice. It was Father Rock.

"May I have permission to speak, Coach?"

Kelly nodded.

Father Rock started to talk.

"Look at you, all of you! Look at each other! What do you see?"

No answers.

"Well, boys, I'll tell you. You see young men from all over the United States. Every state in the Union. You're from different backgrounds, different races, even different religions. You share one thing in common at the moment. You are each wearing the golden helmets and the gold and blue uniforms of the University of Notre Dame. As different as you are, you all share a common heritage. One you seemed to forget in the first half."

Rockne had discovered a videocassette recorder earlier that week and had been fascinated. Great coaching device. He recalled a videotape he knew they had all seen.

"How many of you have ever seen WAKE UP THE ECHOES! Didn't NFL Films do a magnificent job of putting together the history of Notre Dame football? Remember the great comebacks by Notre

Dame? The 1935 win against Ohio State? The 1978 Cotton Bowl comeback led by Joe Montana?"

They were listening intently.

"Well, my favorite part of that film comes at the end. The narrator's voice said these words: 'The spirit of Notre Dame is more than yellowed newspaper clippings and flickering newsreels. It is kept fresh and vibrant by kids from all over America who come to South Bend to live out their dreams. The spirit is not a figment of their imagination. It is real...binding forever past to present, and all those who have felt it.' "

Hart Collins felt goose bumps quivering on his forearms.

Father Rock went on.

"Yes, men. All those who have felt it. Men like George Gipp. Frank Leahy. Ara Parseghian. Moose Krause."

He paused. The secret of public speaking success lay in how one mastered silence.

"Now, I'm not going to tell you to win one for the Gipper. It's already been done – once by Notre Dame and twice by the Republicans."

The boys laughed.

"I'm not going to dress you in brand new jerseys or read you telegrams from Coach Kelly's little kids."

"I'm not going to tell you about Notre Dame's 11 national championships* and six Heisman Trophy winners*. I'm not going to tell you about football at all. Indeed, I'm going to tell you the story of

121

Notre Dame's greatest comeback...when the spirit of Notre Dame was forged forever."

All in the locker room fixed their gaze on Father Rock.

"On April 23, 1879, fire broke out on the Notre Dame campus. Within hours, the main building and four adjacent structures lay in ruins. The University of Notre Dame was all but destroyed.

"The founder of the university, Father Edward Sorin, was 65 years old at the time. Imagine poor Father Sorin stumbling through the ashes, charred beams and smoldering brick that had been his life's work. He had started Notre Dame as a young man, 37 years before. Imagine how he felt. Many lesser men would have quit.

"But you know what? Characteristically, he took the fire as a sign his vision had been too small. That he had dreamed too small a dream for Notre Dame. He reportedly said: "If it were all gone, I should not give up!"

For emphasis, Rockne repeated Sorin's words.

"If it were all gone, I should not give up!"

"Gentlemen, Father Sorin's dream was shattered, but he didn't quit! He told the students go home for the summer, and promised them there would be a new Notre Dame come September. Some of them must have thought the old man was crazy. But he enlisted the help of a Chicago architect and had a new building design in three weeks. He sought help from Chicago and South Bend. A construction marathon ensued. In about four months,

122

without the help of modern construction equipment, Father Sorin and others like him rebuilt Notre Dame.

"Now, Father Sorin had dreamed of a tribute to Our Lady for many years. He once said, 'If all men fail me, there is one treasury that is always full, that of our Most Holy Lady. When this school shall grow a bit more, I shall raise her aloft so that, without asking, all men shall know why we have succeeded here. To that lovely lady, raised high on a dome, a golden dome, men may look and find the answer.'

"Remember the first time your father drove you up Notre Dame Avenue and you saw that golden dome? It's usually at that precise moment, which so many of you have shared, that young men and women first know, really know, that Notre Dame is a very special place.

"The Golden Dome is a symbol of excellence. Of courage. Of devotion. You young men are wearing the golden helmets of the Fighting Irish of Notre Dame – the same gold that covers your beloved dome. It isn't a gold that lights up the skies; it's a gold that lights up the heart.

"Just remember that when you put on those golden helmets of Notre Dame, the true spirit of Notre Dame lies in never giving up, in setting standards of excellence and then measuring up to or perhaps even exceeding them."

Rockne paused once more.

"Gentlemen, there are 30 minutes of football left. If you're in need of a standard, I'll give you one. Twenty-five points. Do you measure up?"

Then he was silent.

Hart Collins had taken a towel. Slowly, almost reverently, he had been rubbing his helmet. He had polished it until it gleamed. He pulled it over his head and firmly fastened the chinstrap.

"Men of Notre Dame, follow me!"

The Fighting Irish of Notre Dame thundered onto the field.

Hart Collins removed any final doubts in the first huddle of the half.

One of the guards had said, "Do you know what the odds are of outscoring USC in the second half? No one, I mean no one, has scored as much as a field goal against them in the second half all season long."

Collins uttered five words.

"Never tell me the odds!"

Collins and his team were now gripped with emotion. He released it with passes to Ryan O'Connor and other Irish receivers.

Shenandoah Lee led a swarming defense that smothered the Trojans time after time. Each time the Trojans attacked, they were repelled.

A flea-flicker turned into a 50 yard gain as the Irish traveled 91 yards on seven plays on their next possession. They added a two-point conversion to make the score USC 24-ND 8.

Shenandoah Lee's defense scored the next two points. The ensuing kickoff had been downed at the USC 2. The Trojans were held for no gain, then a one yard loss. On third and eleven, the quarterback was sacked in the end zone.

USC 24-ND 10.

The Irish got the ball back. Another victory march. Collins scored the touchdown. The PAT was good.

USC 24-ND 17.

The defense had become a wall. Again, USC was forced to punt.

Notre Dame took possession. Collins led another drive.

Making up for lost time now, Collins fired six consecutive strikes from a shotgun formation. From the USC three, he hit O'Connor over the middle. Touchdown!

The Trojans grew dangerous. The try for two was stopped by a savage assault of USC linebackers.

USC 24-ND 23.

On the Irish sideline, Father Rock said to Dutch, "Darn! We'll hear about that one. God just hates it when Catholics foul up conversion attempts!"

Dutch was optimistic. "Relax, Rock. A field goal will win it."

That is, if Notre Dame made the next field goal.

USC powered its way into Notre Dame territory. The Trojans kept the ball on the ground, stripping precious minutes from the clock. The line play became a bruising, punishing struggle as the

Notre Dame defenders attempted to steal the ball away from the surehanded USC tailback, Rocket Crockett.

Crockett breaks free! A game-saving tackle by Shenandoah Lee!

First and goal from the Notre Dame four.

Three times USC battered at Notre Dame's defensive wall, and three times "Our Lady's Tough Guys" slammed them back. Freshman middle linebacker Moose Carrigan, substituting for the injured Dutch Reagan on defense, caught Crockett in mid-air when he tried to use his center as a trampoline and leap into the end zone.

USC went for the sure field goal. It was good!

So close! And now USC had increased its lead to four.

USC still had to kick the ball. There might be time for one last play. Probably only one.

In an unusual move, Coach Kelly sent Collins, the best scrambler on the team, in to receive.

The ball rose and fell to earth. It tumbled toward Collins.

To his left, he saw Shenandoah Lee go down under the onslaught of USC rushers. Crafty Troy Achilles was taking no chances on a lateral.

Collins raced for the ball. If it rolled out of bounds, the game could be over.

It was all up to Hart Collins now, alone at the Notre Dame one.

He lowered his head and charged the two Trojans coming at him full speed. He knocked one out of bounds and wriggled free of the other.

He scrambled to his left. Four yards down, only ninety-five to go.

Ahead of him, the Irish battled Trojans.

Three red jerseys approached. He fled for the protection of blue ones.

"No clips, guys," he yelled, "No penalties."

Collins and his remaining blockers crossed the 50 into USC turf.

The Trojans had nearly overcommitted. There might be a chance.

They crossed the 30, near the west sideline. The 20. The Notre Dame Band was seated almost directly above them.

The band struck up the Victory March.

Collins and his blockers heard it. Emotions surged within them and energy with it. With renewed purpose, they advanced toward the goal. One by one, Collins' blockers went down, but each man took an opponent with him. Moose Carrigan was the last to fall, at the 10.

Only "Raging Bull" Karlson, USC's three time All American gorilla, and his 255 pounds of solid muscle stood between 6 foot 2 inch 185 pound Hart Collins and a Notre Dame victory!

Out of the corner of his eye, Collins glimpsed the figure of Dutch Reagan, leaning on his crutches. He heard Dutch call to him.

"Do it for the old Gipper!"

Collins turned "Raging Bull" into sitting Bull.

He regained his balance and sprinted to the end zone.

TOUCHDOWN NOTRE DAME!

No time remained on the clock. The final score was ND 29-USC 27.

A joyous celebration surrounded Hart Collins. The campus was bathed in a golden light. If one looked hard enough, one could detect a slight smile on the face of Touchdown Jesus as he overlooked the stadium from the mural covering the south face of the Memorial Library.

Knute Rockne tapped Dutch Reagan on the shoulder.

"It's time to go, George," he said, "Our job is done."

"But Rock, what about the bowl game..."

"Sorry, George, but God wants to meet you right away. He wants to get you started on your next mission. It's a permanent assignment. I think you'll like it."

Dutch looked longingly at the pressbox. "Is there enough time to say goodby to Nicki?"

"I wish there was, George."

Rockne looked up and waved. In a flash of heavenly light, Knute Rockne and George Gipp vanished from the earth.

EPILOG

In a stirring Sugar Bowl victory, Notre Dame tamed the Tigers of LSU by a score of 49-0. Ten consecutive wins, one opening day loss and a thrilling early season tie were enough to capture the hearts of the fans and the votes of the pollsters. Notre Dame was the unanimous choice as National Champion.

Coach Joe Kelly was voted Coach of the Year.

Hart Collins went on the become Notre Dame's next Heisman Trophy winner – and the first to win it twice.

Alumni contributions increased dramatically. The Monogram Club – whose membership included all of Notre Dame's varsity letterpersons – raised enough to build a new dormitory, Gipp Hall.

God rewarded the soul of Knute Rockne with "eternal Notre Dame tickets" located on a small cloud circling the earth in a stationary orbit directly above Notre Dame Stadium.

The following year, the Chicago Cubs finally won the World Series. A rookie centerfielder hit 70 home runs, and was voted the National League's Most Valuable Player and Rookie of the Year.

He hit five home runs in the last game of the series. The fourth homer struck one of Wrigley Field's useless banks of lights. The Wrigley Field lights had been mysteriously damaged by lightning the first night they were switched on, and, despite proper repairs, had never functioned again. God later admitted to Rockne that he had day baseball in the back of his mind right from the beginning. ""When I said 'Let there be light,' I meant sunshine! So when the Supreme Court struck down Chicago's city ordinance prohibiting lights, I simply bided My time and struck down the lights themselves," he had said.

The day after the Series ended, the rookie married WGN Television's beautiful young sports journalist, Nicki Summers, consummating a whirlwind summer romance which began when the super, natural Cubs outfielder had knocked a panel out of her apartment door to deliver a dozen peach-colored roses.

The wedding napkins were inscribed, Dutch and Nicki.

The Gipper's Ghost, it appears, had found his Heaven on Earth.

THE END

ABOUT THE AUTHOR

Originally published in 1985, *THE GIPPER'S GHOST* is the first novel written by Robert Quakenbush (pronounced QUAKE -n - bush).

Bob is a Notre Dame graduate. He earned his bachelor's degree in business administration from the University of Notre Dame in 1976. While at Notre Dame, he polished his writing skills as a reporter for the student newspaper, The Observer, and as sports editor of the 1975 yearbook, The Dome. He also served as chairman of Notre Dame's annual springtime festival, An Tostal.

The Muncie, Indiana, native was raised in the northwest suburbs of Detroit, where he attended and graduated from Our Lady Queen of Martyrs grade school and Brother Rice High School.

He spent many years in Chicago as a public relations and marketing communications professional.

Despite what he himself calls "the highly questionable theology" presented in *THE GIPPER'S GHOST*, Bob later handled media relations for the Roman Catholic Archdiocese of Chicago, and was even appointed Chief Communications Officer by its archbishop, the late Joseph Cardinal Bernardin, proving once again that God has a sense of humor and works in strange and mysterious ways!

In recent years, Bob has been primarily involved with educational institutions, engaged in marketing communications in support of major fundraising efforts. He worked in campaign communications at Culver Academies in Culver, Indiana, promoting the school's highly successful *By Example* campaign, served on the school board for Saint Joseph High School in South Bend, Indiana, and served as assistant director for development marketing communications at his alma mater, the University of Notre Dame.

Today, he lives his life with his wife Mary Beth, daughter Kelly, and their small dogs in Cary, North Carolina.

EXPLANATORY NOTES

Page 6: "1977 Chevrolets"

When *The Gipper's Ghost* was written in 1985, eight years seemed like such a very long time since 1977, when Notre Dame had last won a national championship. But in 2014, you could add "rusty 1988 Chevrolets" to the sentence, since it has now been 26 years since the Fighting Irish last won the national championship.

Page 7: "fateful day in March, 1931"

Knute Rockne and seven others were killed in an airplane crash on March 31, 1931, when their wooden-winged Fokker Trimotor airliner crashed into the Kansas prairie while on its way to Los Angeles.

Page 43: "Room 305"

Built in 1939 as a men's residence hall, Breen-Phillips Hall became a women's residence hall in the fall of 1973. The author of *The Gipper's Ghost* himself lived in Room 305 during his freshman year (1972-73) - the first year of coeducation at Notre Dame, and the last year Breen-Phillips served as a men's residence hall.

Page 49: "59,075 assistant coaches"

The official capacity of Notre Dame Stadium in 1985 was 59,075. An expansion of the stadium completed before the 1997 season kickoff added more than 21,000 seats, increasing capacity to its present-day 80,795.

Page 49: "statistics"

The statistics on page 49 were accurate when the book was published in 1985 and reflected Notre Dame's first 95 seasons of football. By the end of the 2013 season, Notre Dame had completed 126 seasons and the football team's record stood at 874-305-42 (874 wins, 305 losses, and 42 ties). Notre Dame had also reclaimed the top spot as the college football team with the highest winning percentage (.733). As of 2014, Notre Dame had completed 106 winning seasons in 126 years of football, and only 13 losing seasons.

Page 121: "11 national championships"

Today (in 2014), Notre Dame generally is considered to have won eleven "consensus" national titles, in 1924, 1929, 1930, 1943, 1946, 1947, 1949, 1966, 1973, 1977, and 1988.

Page 121: "six Heisman Trophy winners."

When the book was published in 1985, Notre Dame took great pride in its six Heisman Trophy winners: Angelo Bertelli (1943), Johnny Lujack (1947), Leon Hart (1949), Johnny Lattner (1953), Paul Hornung (1956), and John Huarte (1964). In 1987, Tim Brown became the seventh Notre Dame player to win the Heisman Trophy.

Shake Down The Thunder!

Go Irish!

GIPPER'S GHOST QUIZ

1. Who is the author of *The Gipper's Ghost?*

2. What was Rockne's disguise in the book?

3. What name did the Gipper adopt when he returned to Notre Dame?

4. In the book, who lived in Room 305 of Breen-Phillips Hall?

5. Which President of the United States played George Gipp in the movie, *Knute Rockne – All American?*

6. Who is the founder of the University of Notre Dame?

7. What is the name of Notre Dame's student newspaper?

8. What are the first five words of the Notre Dame Victory March?

9. What are the last four words of Notre Dame's alma mater?

10. What is the "tenth and most important commandment" of Notre Dame football?

BONUS QUESTION: Name one of the last three male students to live in Room 305 of Breen-Phillips Hall in 1972-73, before B-P was converted to a women's dorm.

If you score 90 percent, you clearly understand the spirit of Notre Dame! If you score less than 90 percent, you need to Study Like A Champion Today!

ANSWERS: 1. Robert A. Quakenbush 2. Priest 3. Dutch Reagan 4. Nicki Summers, the sports editor of The Observer 5. Ronald Reagan 6. Rev. Edward F. Sorin, C.S.C. 7. The Observer 8. Rally sons of Notre Dame 9. Love thee, Notre Dame 10. Thou Shalt Never Lose to USC

Bonus Question: John Carrico, Harold "Hank" Gilday, or Bob Quakenbush, all proud members of the Notre Dame Class of 1976.

P.T. Brent L4
1350 Ala Moana Boulevard
Honolulu, Hawaii 96814
808-545-2929 • ptb2929@gmail.com

Made in the USA
San Bernardino, CA
21 October 2014

16171209R00088